THE COMPREHENSIVE
STUDY OF MUSIC
ANTHOLOGY OF MUSIC FROM
BEETHOVEN THROUGH WAGNER

THE COMPREHENSIVE STUDY OF MUSIC
ANTHOLOGY OF MUSIC FROM BEETHOVEN THROUGH WAGNER

William Brandt
WASHINGTON STATE UNIVERSITY

Arthur Corra
ILLINOIS STATE UNIVERSITY

William Christ

Richard DeLone

Allen Winold
INDIANA UNIVERSITY

HARPER'S COLLEGE PRESS

A Department of Harper & Row, Publishers
NEW YORK   HAGERSTOWN   SAN FRANCISCO   LONDON

78502

Brunnhilde's "Immolation" from Die Gotterdammerung *by Wilhelm Richard Wagner, piano transcription by Karl Klindworth. Courtesy of G. Schirmer, Inc.*

Coronation Scene from Boris Godunov *by Modest Petrovich Moussorgsky, Paul Lamm, editor, translation by David Lloyd-Jones. Reprinted by permission of Oxford University Press.*

For information address Harper & Row, Publishers, Inc. 10 East 53rd Street, New York, N.Y. 10022.

Library of Congress Catalog Number: 75-19402
ISBN: 0-06-161422-X

CONTENTS

THE COMPREHENSIVE
STUDY OF MUSIC
ANTHOLOGY OF MUSIC FROM
BEETHOVEN THROUGH WAGNER

SONATA, OP. 10, NO. 3

THIRD MOVEMENT
Fourth

 LUDWIG VAN BEETHOVEN

Rondo
Allegro

[5]

[10]

[15]

[20]

4   *Ludwig van Beethoven*

[75]

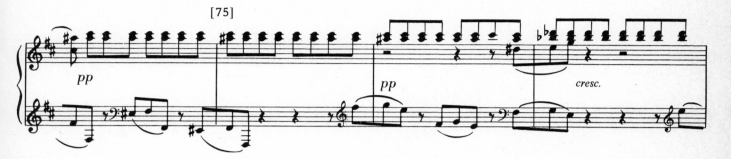

[80]

[85]

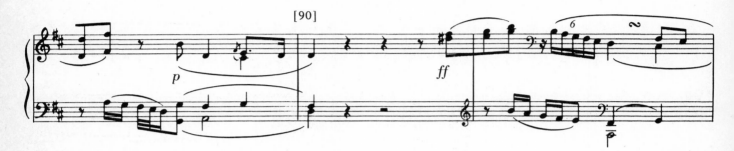

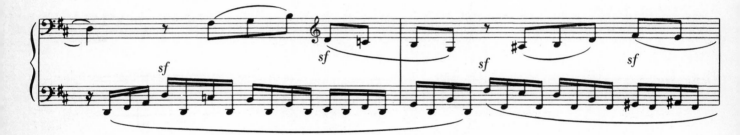

STRING QUARTET, OP. 127, NO. 12

FIRST MOVEMENT

LUDWIG VAN BEETHOVEN

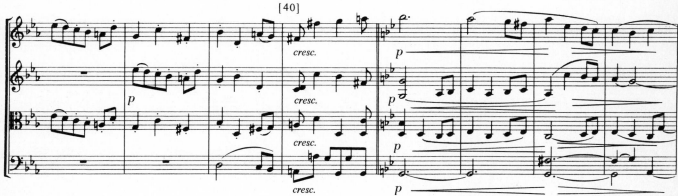

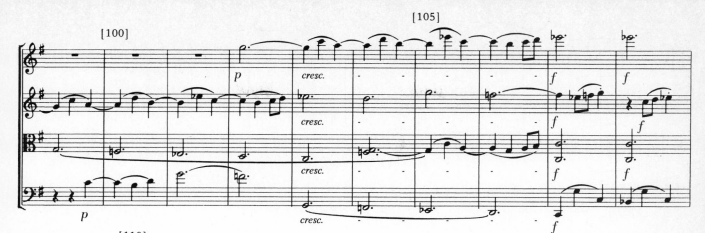

Maestoso [135]

Allegro [140]　　　　　　　　　　[145]

[150]　　　　　　　　　　[155]

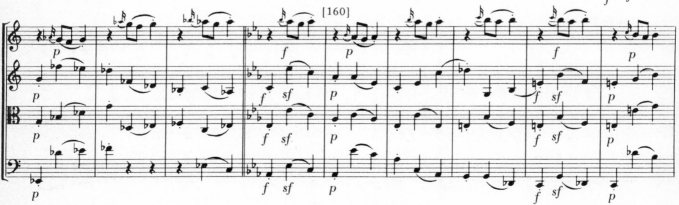

[160]

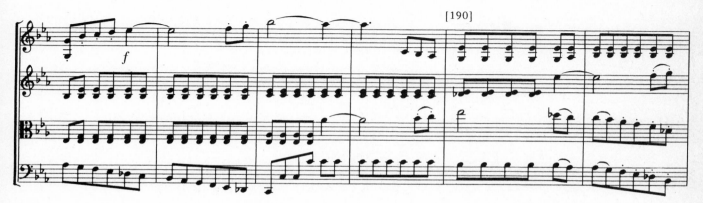

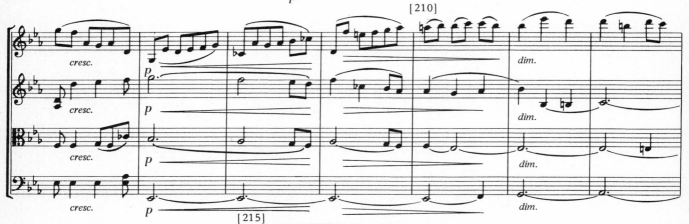

Scherzando vivace

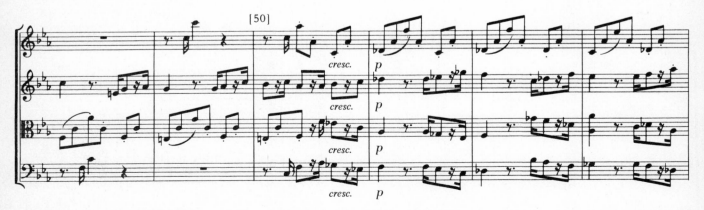

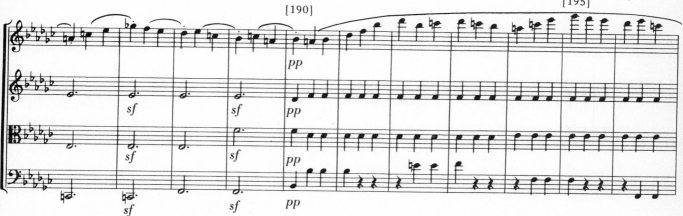

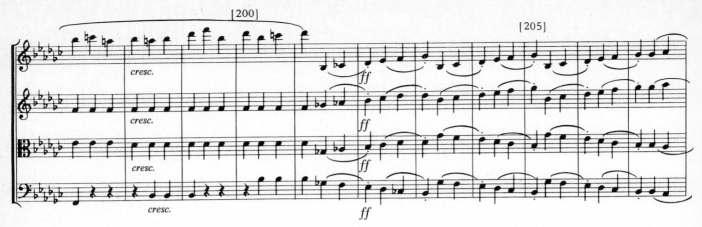

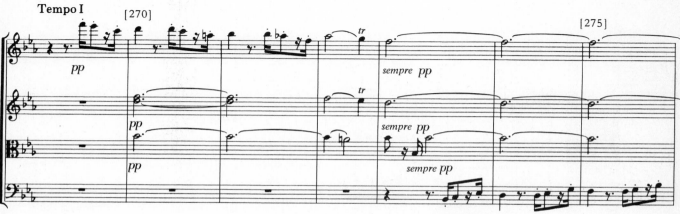

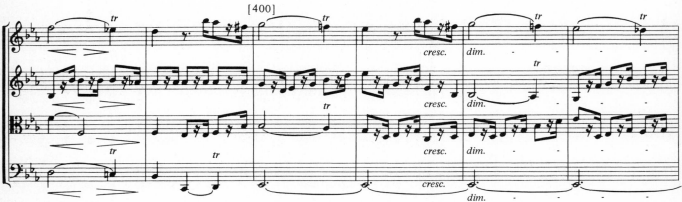

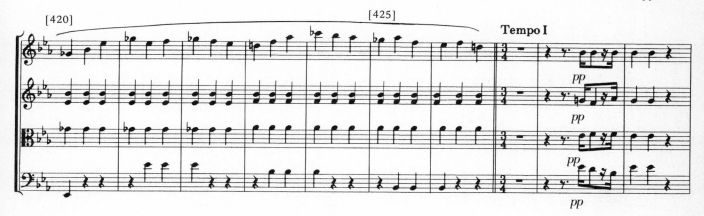

SYMPHONY NO. 3, OP. 55

FIRST MOVEMENT

LUDWIG VAN BEETHOVEN

Development

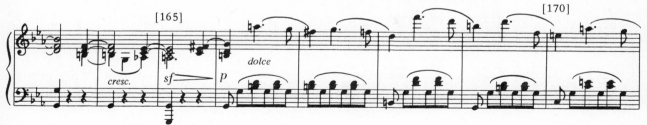

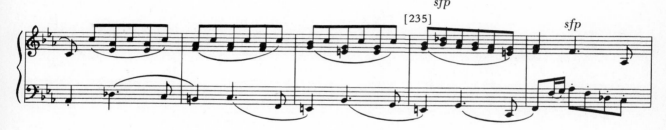

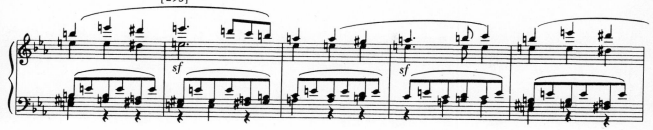

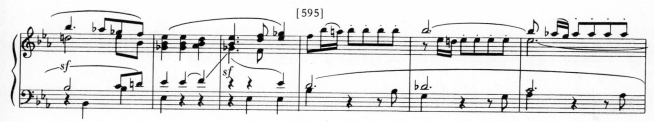

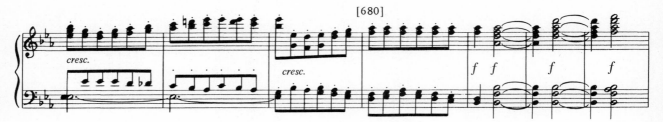

FINALE
Allegro molto

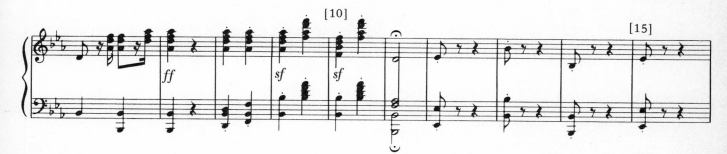

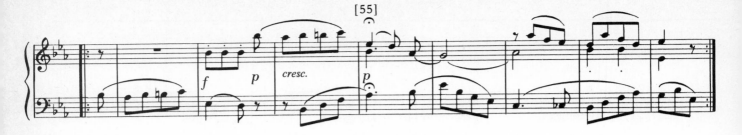

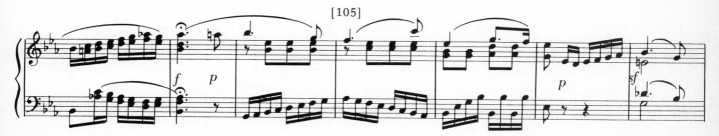

SYMPHONY NO. 3   67

72   *Ludwig van Beethoven*

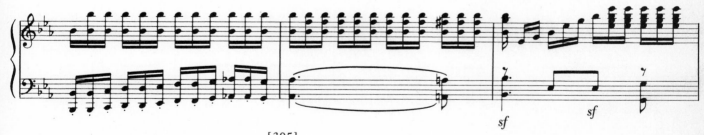

[445]

[450]

[455]

[460]

[465]

[470]

THE BARBER OF SEVILLE

CAVATINA: "LARGO AL FACTOTUM DELLA CITTA"

GIOACCHINO ROSSINI

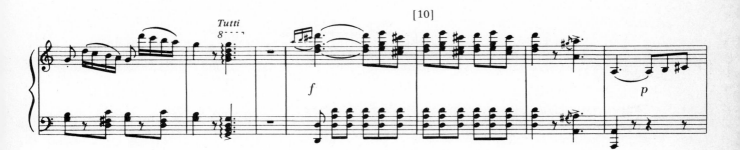

la la le ra,
la ran la

le ra,
la ran la la.

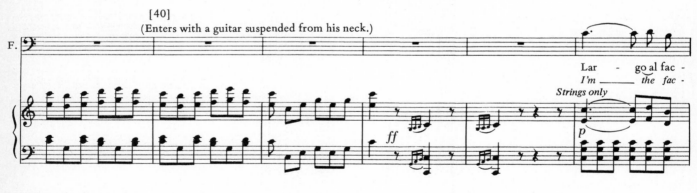

(Enters with a guitar suspended from his neck.)

Lar - go al fac -
I'm ___ the fac -
Strings only

to - tum del - la cit - tà,
lar - go!
La ran la la ran la la ran
to - tum of all the town,
at
large!

F. Pronto a far
Ready for

F. tut - to, la not-te il gior - no sem-pre d'in - tor - no in gi - ro sta. Mi-glior cuc -
anything, night or day *Noth-ing can tire me, read - y for all. Of all pro -*

F. ca - gna per un bar - bie - re, vi - ta più no - bi - le, no, non si da. La le ran
fes - sions that you can name That of a bar - ber is best of them all.

Fag. & Strings

[120]

F. la le ran la le ran la le ran la le ran la le ran la le ran la.

cresc.

Ra - so - ri e
Razors and

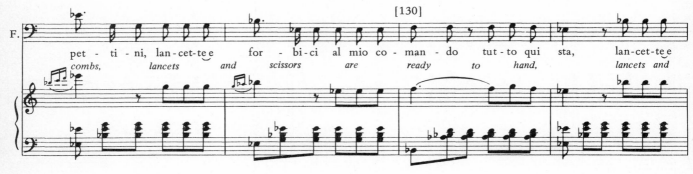

pet - ti - ni, lan - cet - te e for - bi - ci al mio co - man - do tut - to qui sta, lan - cet - te e
combs, lancets and scissors are ready to hand, lancets and

for - bi - ci, ra - so - ri e pet - ti - ni al mio co - man - do tut - to qui sta.
scissors, razors and combs all stand ready to hand,

Vè la ri - sor - sa poi del me - sti - ere col - la don - net -
Behold the resources, then, of the profession with the young ladies,

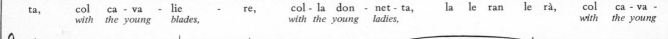

ta, col ca - va - lie - re, col - la don - net - ta, la le ran le rà, col ca - va -
with the young blades, with the young ladies, with the young

WOHIN?

FRANZ PETER SCHUBERT

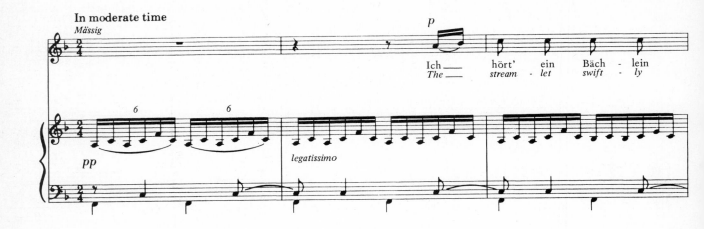

In moderate time
Mässig

Ich____ hört' ein Bäch - lein
The____ stream - let swift - ly

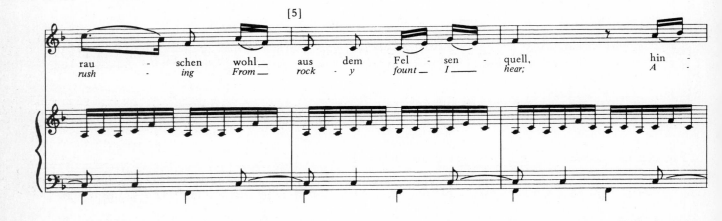

[5]

rau - schen wohl__ aus dem Fel - sen - quell, hin -
rush - ing From__ rock - y fount I__ hear; A -

ab zum Tha - le rau - schen so__ frisch und wun - der -
down the vale are dash - ing Its__ wa - ters bright__ and__

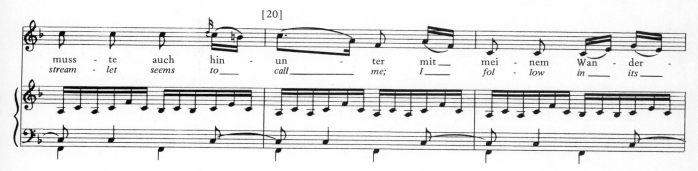

[40]

hin?_____ sprich, wo — hin?_____ Du hast mit dei — nem
say,_____ whith — er say?_____ The mur — mur of thy

[45]

Rau — schen mir ganz be — rauscht den Sinn, du
wa — ters Doth steal my wits a — way; The

hast mit dei — nem__ Rau — schen mir ganz be — rauscht__ den
mur — mur of____ thy__ wa ters Doth__ steal my wits____ a —

[50]

Sinn. Was sag' ich denn vom Rau — schen? das
way; Me — thinks tis not the mur — mur Of

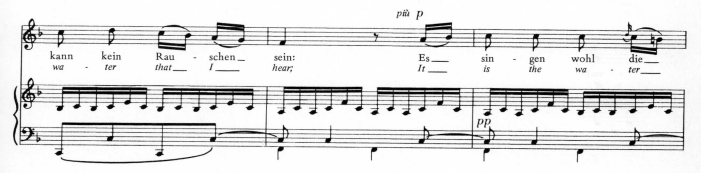

kann kein Rau — schen__ sein: Es__ sin — gen wohl die
wa ter that__ I____ hear; It__ is the wa — ter____

Ni - xen tief___ un - ten ih - ren Reih'n, es___
nix - ies Whose___ song doth charm___ mine___ ear, *It___*

sin - gen wohl die Ni - xen tief___ un - ten ih - ren
is the wa - ter___ nix - ies Whose___ song doth charm___ mine___

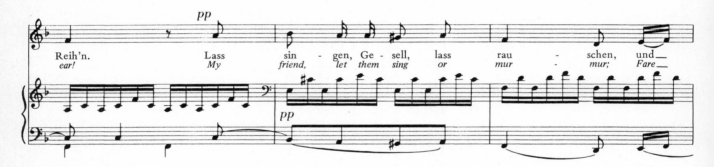

Reih'n. Lass sin - gen, Ge - sell, lass rau - schen, und
ear! My friend, let them sing or mur - mur; Fare___

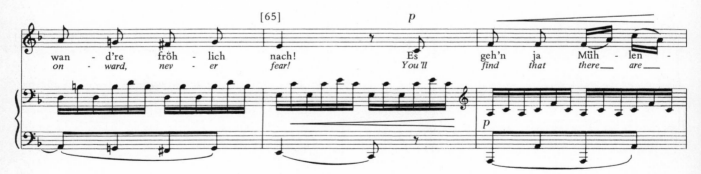

wan - d're fröh - lich nach! Es geh'n ja Müh - len -
on - ward, nev - er fear! You'll find that there___ are___

rä - der in___ je - dem kla - ren___ Bach,___ es
mill - wheels In___ ev - 'ry stream - let___ clear!___ You'll

92   *Franz Peter Schubert*

geh'n ja Müh - len - rä - der_ in_ je - dem kla - ren_
find that there_ are_ mill - wheels_ In_ ev - 'ry stream - let

Bach. Lass_ sin - gen, Ge - sell,_ lass_ rau - schen, und_
*clear! My_ friend, let them sing_ or_ mur - mur; Fare_*

wan - d're fröh - lich_ nach, fröh - lich_ nach, fröh - lich
on - ward, nev - er_ fear! Nev - er_ fear! Nev - er

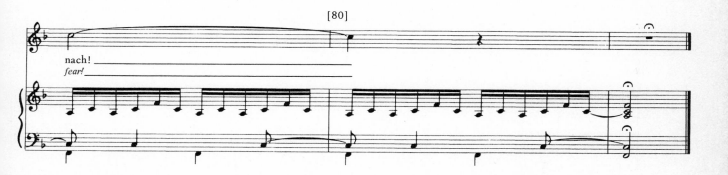

nach! _____
fear! _____

DER DOPPELGANGER

FRANZ PETER SCHUBERT

Heine

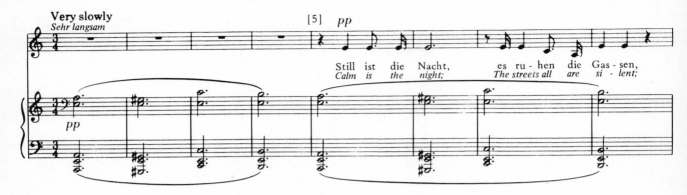

Still ist die Nacht, es ru - hen die Gas - sen,
Calm is the night; The streets all are si - lent;

in die - sem Hau - se wohn - te mein Schatz; sie hat schon
This house she dwelt in, She, I lov'd dear; Tis long a -

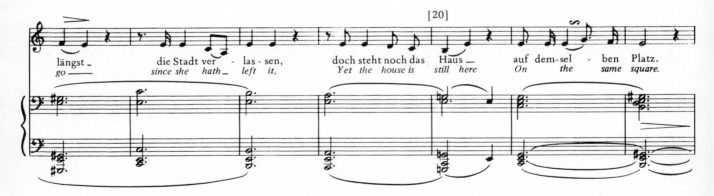

längst die Stadt ver - las - sen, doch steht noch das Haus auf dem-sel - ben Platz.
go since she hath left it, Yet the house is still here On the same square.

Da steht auch ein Mensch, und starrt in die Hö - he,
Here, too, stands a man who sky - ward is gaz - ing,

DER LINDENBAUM

FRANZ PETER SCHUBERT

Wort;   es zog in Freud'und Lei - de zu ihm __ mich im - mer fort.
fair;   *When joy was mine, or sor - row, I found __ my so - lace there!*

Ich
E'en

musst' auch heu - te wan - dern vor - bei in tie - fer Nacht,   da
now had I to pass it, A - lone, in dark - est night;   *And*

hab' ich noch im Dun - kel die Au - gen zu - ge - macht.   Und
lest I should be - hold it I co - ver'd up __ my sight.   *It's*

sei - ne Zwei - ge rausch - ten, als rie - fen sie mir zu: komm'
wav - ing branch - es whis - per'd A mes - sage in my ear; And

her zu mir, Ge - sel - le, hier find'st du dei - ne Ruh!
said: "Come hith - er, com - rade. For rest and peace are here!"

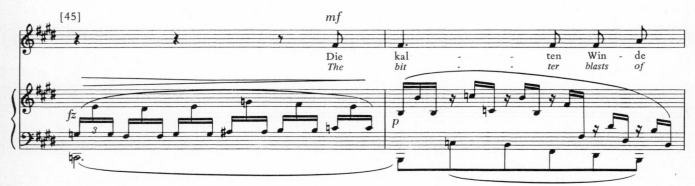

Die kal - ten Win - de
The bit - ter blasts of

blie - sen mir grad' in's An - ge -
win - ter They smite up - on my

sicht, der Hut flog mir vom
brow; Yet I must face the

Ko - pfe, ich wen - de - te mich
tem - pest; Re - turn I can - not

nicht.
now!

[55]

[60]

Nun bin ich man - che Stun - de ent - fernt von je - nem
Aye, on - ward, ev - er on - ward! While ev - er in my

[65]

Ort, und im - mer hör' ich's rau - schen: du fän - dest Ru - he
ear The lin - den's mes - sage lin - gers: "Lo! rest and peace are

STRING QUARTET IN G MAJOR, OP. 161, (D. 887)

FIRST MOVEMENT

FRANZ PETER SCHUBERT

[135]

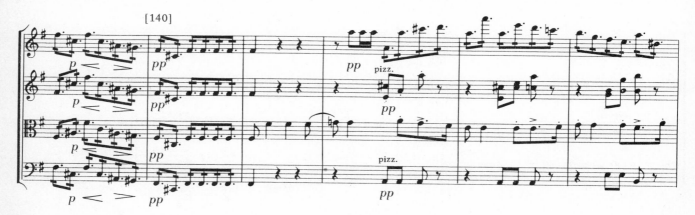

[140]

[145]

[150]

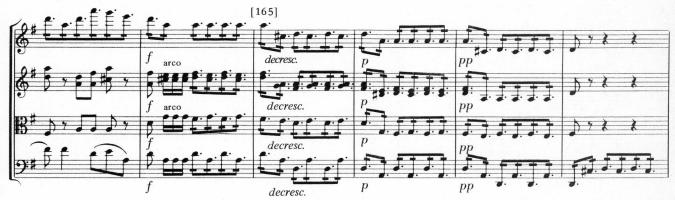

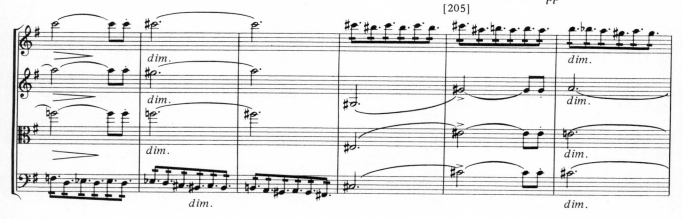

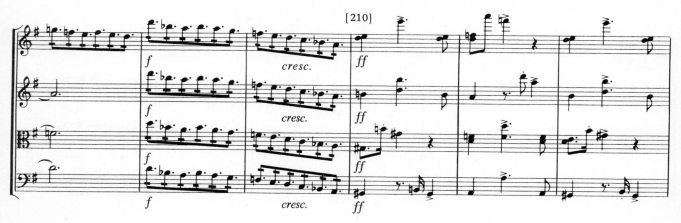

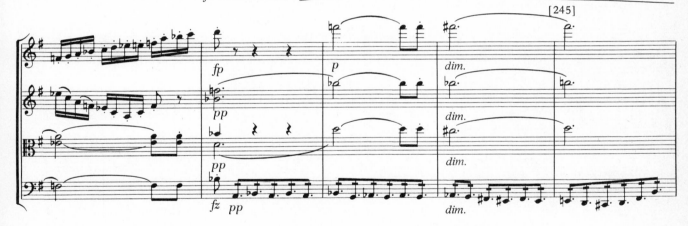

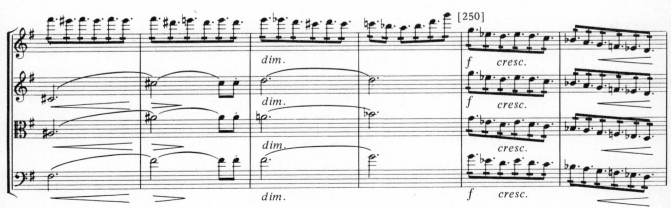

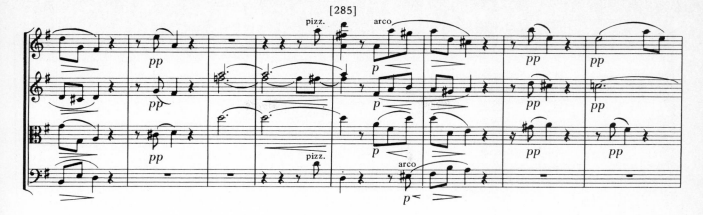

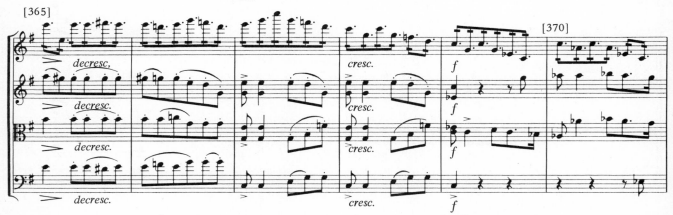

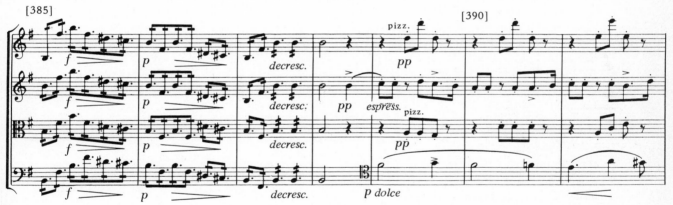

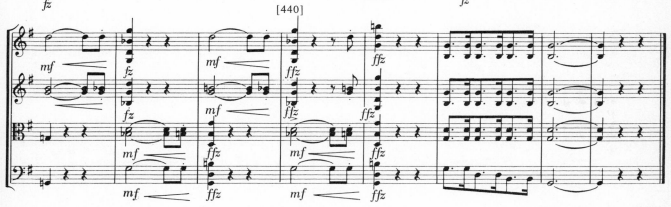

LE SPECTRE DE LA ROSE

HECTOR BERLIOZ

Adagio un poco lento e dolce assai

Piano

pp

[5]

dolce assai e

Sou -
Raise

[10] *placido*

lè - ve ta pau-piè - re clo - se Qu'ef-fleure un
your closed eyelids . . . . gently touched

son — ge vir - gi - nal! _____ Je
by a virginal dream *I*

suis le spec - tre d'u — ne ro - se, Que tu por -
am the spirit of a _____ rose, Which you

tais, _____ hi - er au bal. Tu me
wore last night at the ball. You took

pris en - core em - per - le - é Des pleurs — d'ar -
me still pearled by the silver

gent   de l'ar - ro - soir,   Et par -
tears   *of the sprinkler,*   *And amidst*

mi _____ la fe - te é - toi -
the brilliant festivities, ... *amidst*

lé - e,   Tu _____ me pro - me -
. . . . *You _____ carried me*

nas,   tu me pro - me - nas   tout _____ le
. . . .   *all _____ evening.*

122   *Hector Berlioz*

[40]

rien, ... Je ne ré - cla - me Ni mes - se
I do not ask *a Mass*

ni De Pro - fun - dis. Ce lé - ger par - fum est mon
nor De Profundis, *This faint perfume is my*

pp

poco cre - scen

â - me, Ce lé - ger par - fum _____ est mon â - me Et j'ar -
soul *and I*

poco cre - scen -

[45] *do* *mf* *cresc.* **poco rall.** *cresc.*

ri - ve, j'ar - ri - ve du pa - ra - dis, _____ J'ar - ri - ve, j'ar -
come, *I come* *from Paradise . . . . . .*

do *mf* *cresc.* *cresc.*

allargando *f* **Tempo I** [50]

ri - ve du pa - ra - dis. _____ Mon des - tin fut
My destiny could

ff *dim.* *pp*

124   *Hector Berlioz*

ROMEO AND JULIET

HECTOR BERLIOZ

Combat - Tumult - Intervention of the Prince.

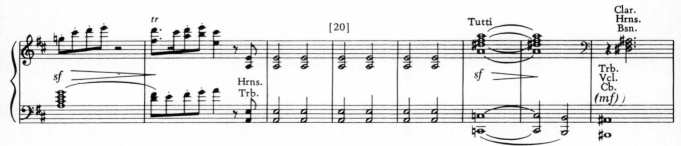

Fieramente, un poco ritenuto, col carattere di Recitative, misurato.

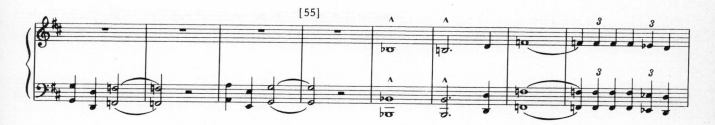

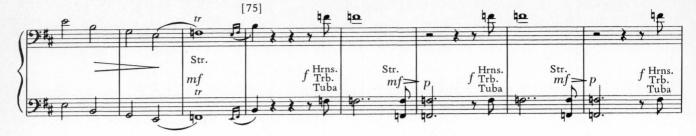

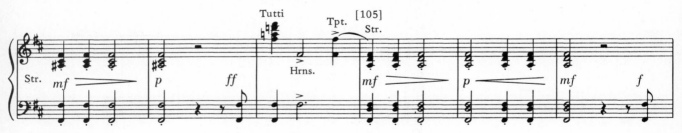

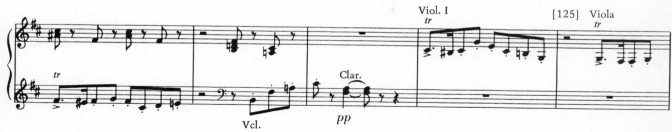

2. Prologue
a) Choral Recitativo

[160]

mi - es, Dans Vé - rone ont croi - sé le fer. Pour - tant de ces sang - lants dé -
ri - ot; an - cient ha - tred bursts in - to flames. Our prince, to stay the dead - ly

sor - dres Le Prince a ré - pri - mé le cours, En me - na - çant de mort ceux
quar - rel, this hate - ful strife, hath made a law stat - ing that he with in - stant

[165]

qui, mal - gré ses or - dres, Aux jus - ti - ces du glaive aur - aient en - cor re -
death shall be pun - ished, who his sword in de - fence of his rights shall

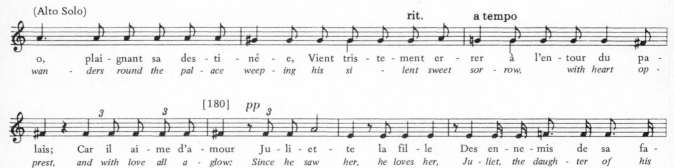

mil - le.
foe. —
Le bruit des ins - tru - ments, les chants mé - lo - di - eux Par - tent des sa - lons où l'or -
The sound of strings is heard, and sweet - est songs en - trance; out from yon halls bright il -

Le bruit des ins - tru - ments, les chants mé - lo - di - eux Par - tent des sa - lons où l'or -
The sound of strings is heard, and sweet - est songs en - trance; out from yon halls bright il -

Le bruit des ins - tru - ments, les chants mé - lo - di - eux Par - tent des sa - lons où l'or -
The sound of strings is heard, and sweet - est songs en - trance; out from yon halls bright il -

Harp

bril - le, ex - ci - tant et la danse et les é - clats joy - eux.
lum - in'd mer - ry voic - es re - sound, on goes the mer - ry dance.

bril - le, ex - ci - tant et la danse et les é - clats joy - eux.
lum - in'd mer - ry voic - es re - sound, on goes the mer - ry dance.

bril - le, ex - ci - tant et la danse et les é - clats joy - eux.
lum - in'd mer - ry voic - es re - sound, on goes the mer - ry dance.

poco ritenuto   Allegro

Fl. Ob. Clar.

Str. (pizz.)

Bsn.

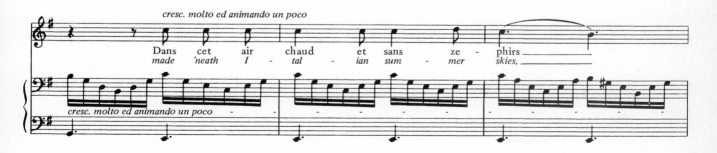

MAZURKA, OP. 17, NO. 4

FREDERIC FRANCOIS CHOPIN

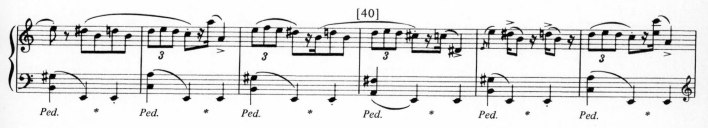

PRELUDE, OP. 28, NO. 17

FREDERIC FRANCOIS CHOPIN

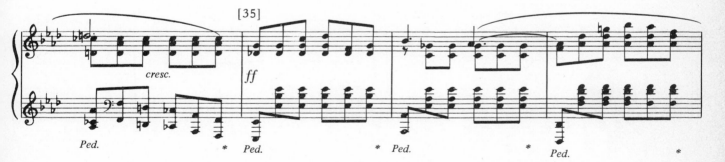

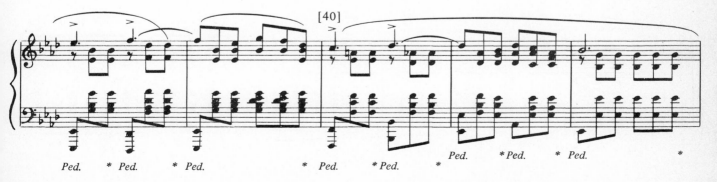

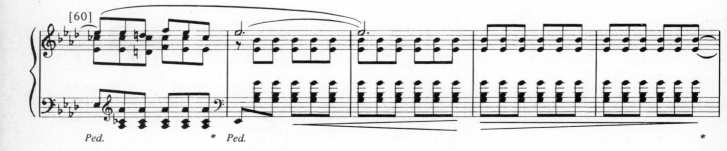

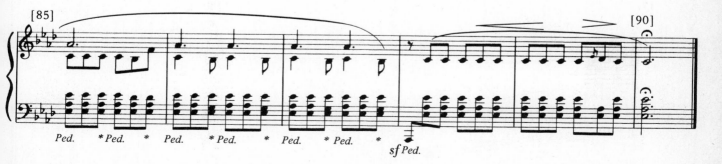

PRELUDE, OP. 28, NO. 18

FREDERIC FRANCOIS CHOPIN

CARNAVAL, OP. 9

EXCERPTS

Scenes mignonnes sur quatre notes*

ROBERT SCHUMANN

Préambule

* A. S. C. H. *The name of a small town in Bohemia where a lady who was a friend of the composer lived.*

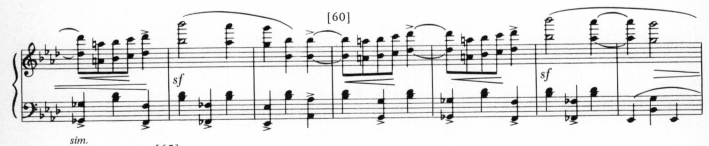

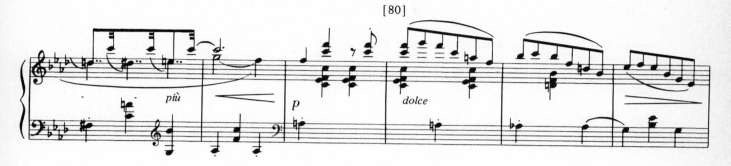

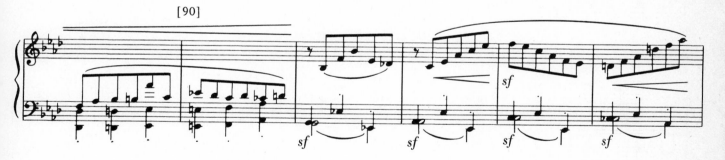

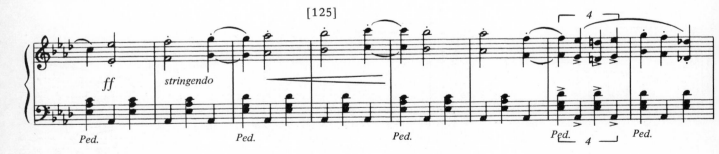

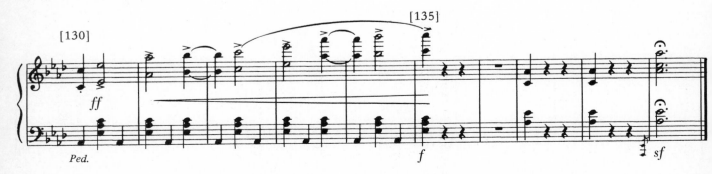

Pierrot

Arlequin

Eusebius

Florestan

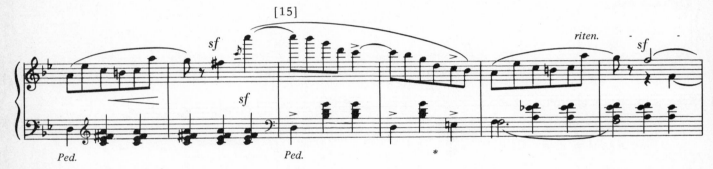

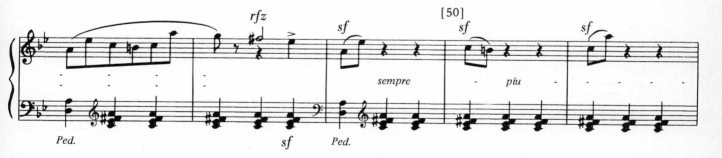

Coquette

Chiarina

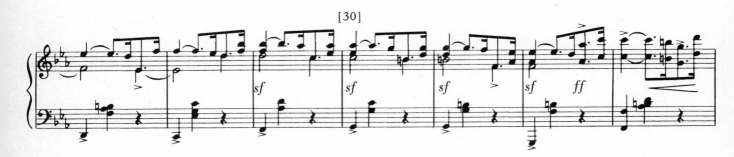

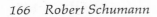

* 2ª volta *pp*

FRAUEN-LIEBE UND LEBEN, OP. 42

I. SEIT ICH IHN GESEHEN

ROBERT SCHUMANN

Seit ich ihn ge - se - hen, glaub' ich
Since I saw him, *I believe*

blind zu sein; wo ich hin nur blik - ke, seh' ich ihn al - lein; wie im
I have become blind; *wherever I look* *I see only him;* *as in*

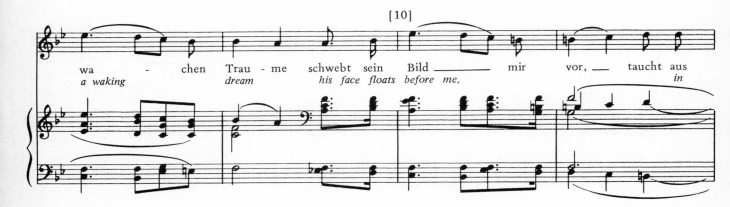

wa - chen Trau - me schwebt sein Bild mir vor, taucht aus
a waking *dream* *his face floats before me,* *in*

tief - stem Dun - kel hel - ler, hel - ler nur em - por.
the deepest *darkness,* *it appears more brightly.*

Sonst ist licht - und farb - los al - les um mich her,
Colorless and pale is everything around me,

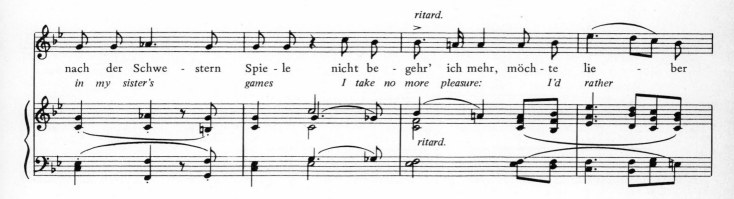

nach der Schwe - stern Spie - le nicht be - gehr' ich mehr, möch - te lie - ber
in my sister's games I take no more pleasure: I'd rather

wei - nen, still im Käm - mer - lein; — seit ich ihn ge - se - hen,
weep quietly in my little room; since I saw him

glaub' ich blind zu sein.
I believe I have become blind.

IV. DU RING AN MEINEM FINGER

Innig.

Du Ring an mei-nem Fin - ger, mein gol-den-es Rin - ge - lein, ich
Thou ring on my finger, my little golden ring,

[5] drük - ke dich fromm an die Lip - pen, dich fromm an die Lip - pen, an das
I press you devoutly to my lips. and to

Her - ze mein. Ich hatt' ihn aus - ge träu - met, der Kind - heit fried - lich [10]
my heart. I had finished that dream of childhood, peaceful

schö - nen Traum, ich fand all-ein mich ver - lo - ren im ö - den un-end - lich-en [15]
land beautiful, I found myself alone, lost in a dreary unending

Ped. *

Raum. Du_ Ring an mei - nem Fin - ger, da_ hast du mich erst be -
space. You, ring on my finger, have taught me,

[20]

lehrt, hast_ mei - nem Blick er schlos - sen des_ Le - bens un -end -lich-en
have unlocked my eyes to life's unending deep

[25]
Nach und nach rascher.

tie - fen Wert. Ich will ihm die - nen, ihm le - ben, ihm
value. I will serve him, live for him, belong

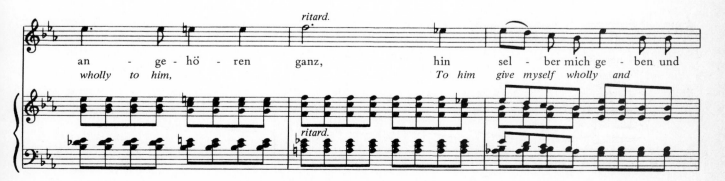

ritard.

an - ge - hö - ren ganz, hin sel - ber mich ge - ben und
wholly to him, To him give myself wholly and

ritard.

[30] *ritard.*

fin - den verk - lärt mich, und fin - den verk - lärt mich in sei - nem Glanz. Du __
find myself transfigured . . . . in his brightness. Thou

ritard.

[35]

Ring an mei - nem Fin - ger, mein__ gol - de - nes Rin - ge - lein, ich __
ring on my finger, my little golden ring, I

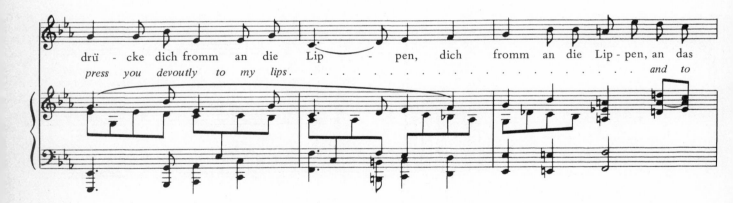

drü - cke dich fromm an die Lip - pen, dich fromm an die Lip - pen, an das
press you devoutly to my lips . . . . and to

[40]

Her - ze mein.
my heart.

Ped. *

[15]

p

mehr.   Ich   zieh' mich in mein Inn' - res   still   zu - rück,   der   Schlei - er
more.   I   draw   back   into   my   inner   silence,   the   veil

[20] *ritardando*

fällt,   da   hab' ich dich und mein ver - lor - nes   Glück,   du   mei - ne   Welt!
falls,   There   I   have   you   and my   lost   happiness,   you,   my   whole   world!

Adagio.   *Tempo wie das erste Lied.* [25]

Ped.   *

[30]

[35]

[40]

174   *Robert Schumann*

SONETTO 123 DEL PETRARCA

FRANZ LISZT

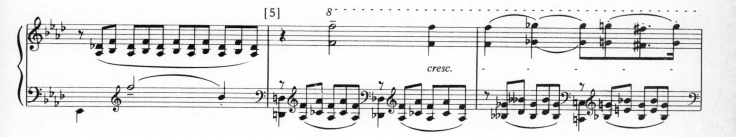

A FAUST SYMPHONY

FIRST MOVEMENT, "FAUST," EXCERPT

FRANZ LISZT

Allegro impetuoso.

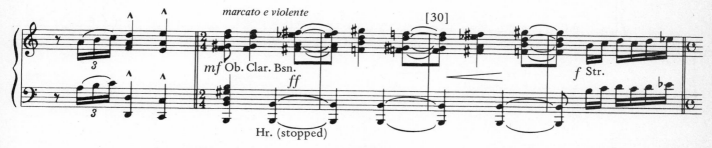

Allegro agitato ed appassionato assai.

[75]

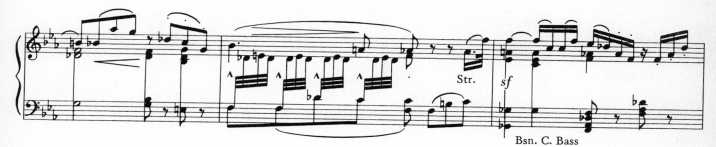

[80] Ob. Bsn.
Str.

Fl.
Clar.
Viol.

[85]

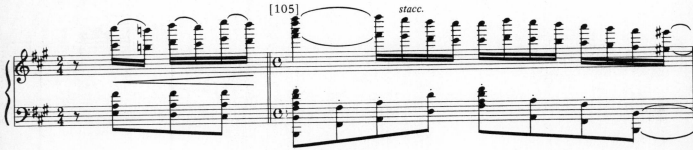

TRISTAN UND ISOLDE

PRELUDE

RICHARD WAGNER

Langsam und schmachtend

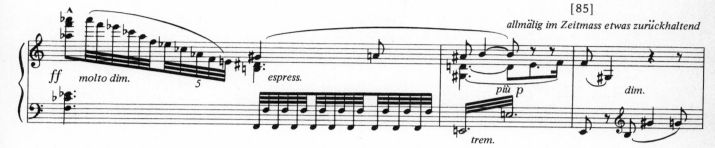

[85]

allmälig im Zeitmass etwas zurückhaltend

[90]

[95]

[100]

[105]

(Der Vorhang geht auf.)

DIE GOTTERDAMMERUNG

BRUNNHILDE'S IMMOLATION

RICHARD WAGNER

(Hagen stands, defiantly leaning on his spear, sunk in gloomy

Immer nachlassend im Zeitmass

[10]

brooding, on the opposite side. — Brünnhilde alone in the center: after remaining long absorbed in contemplation of Sieg-

molto ritard.

fried she turns now to the men and women with solemn exaltation.)

Sehr breit und langsamer als zuvor.

[15] *marcato*

marcato

BRÜNNH. *(to the Vassals)*

Star - ke schei - te schich - tet mir
Might - y logs I bid you now

BRÜNNH.

[20]

dort am Ran - de des Rhein's zu Hauf'!
pile on high by the riv - er shore!

Hoch und hell lod' - re die
Bright and fierce kin - dle a

[25]

Gluth, die den ed - - - len
fire; let the no - - - blest

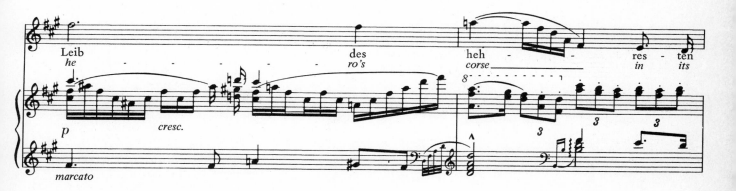

Leib des heh - - - res - ten
he - ro's corse in its

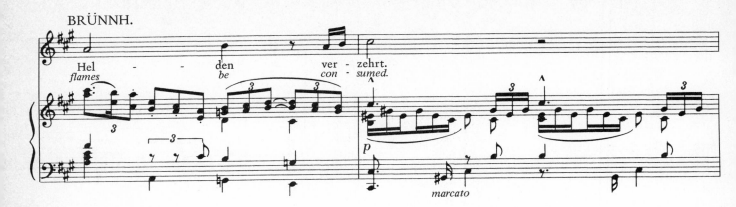

Hel — den ver-zehrt.
flames be con - sumed.

[30]

Sein Ross füh — ret da-her, dass mit
His steed bring to me here, that with

mir dem Re — cken es fol — ge: denn des
me his lord he may fol - low: for my

[35]

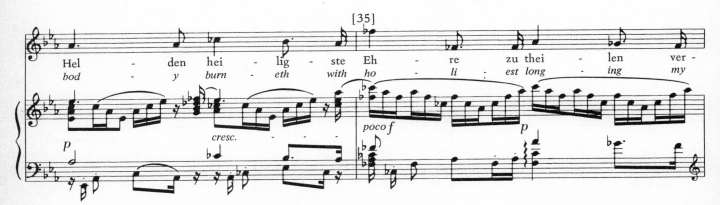

Hel — den hei - lig - ste Eh — re zu thei - len ver-
bod - y burn - eth with ho - li - est long - ing my

194   *Richard Wagner*

langt mein ei - ge-ner Leib.
he - ro's hon - our to share.

Voll - bringt
Ful - fill

During the following the young men raise a huge funeral pyre
of logs before the hall, near the bank of the Rhine: women

[40]

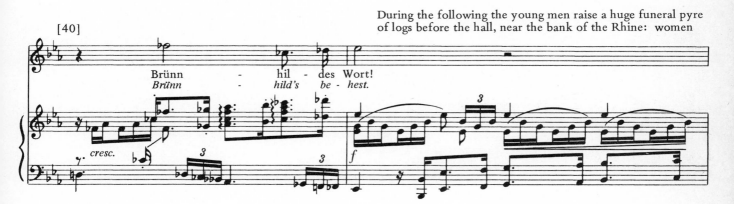

Brünn - hil - des Wort!
Brünn - hild's be - hest.

decorate this with coverings on which
they strew plants and flowers.)   (Brünnhilde becomes again absorbed in contemplation of Siegfried's dead face.)

(Her features take gradually a softer and brighter expression.)   [50]

Wie   Son   -   ne lan   -   ter strahlt   mir sein
Like   rays   of   sun   -   shine stream   -   -   eth   his

[55]

Licht,   der Rein   -   -   ste
light: the   pur   -   -   est

196   *Richard Wagner*

BRÜNNH.

war er, _____ der mich ver - rieth! Die Gat - tin trü - gend
was he _____ *who hath be - trayed!* *In wed - lock trai - tor*

[60]

treu dem Freun - de, vor der eig' - nen Trau - ten ein - - zig ihm
true in friend - ship, *from his heart's own true - love* *on - - ly be -*

[65]

theu - - er, schied er sich durch sein Schwert.
loved - - one, *barred was he* *by his sword.*

Äch - ter als er schwur Kei - ner Ei - de; treu - er als er hielt Kei - ner Ver -
Tru - er than his were oaths ne'er spo - ken; *faith - ful as he, none ev - er held*

BRÜNNH.

[70]

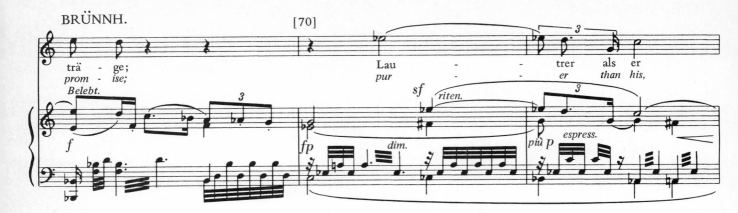

trä - ge;
prom - ise;
Belebt.
f

Lau - - trer als er
pur - - er than his,
sf *riten.*
fp *dim.* *più p* *espress.*

lieb - te kein And' - rer:
love ne'er was plight - ed:
ancora più rit. - - -
più p
f *fp*

Und doch, al - le
Yet oaths hath he

[75]

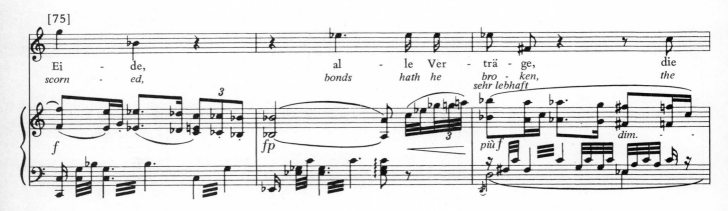

Ei - de,
scorn - ed,
f

al - le Ver - trä - ge,
bonds hath he bro - ken,
sehr lebhaft
fp *più f* *dim.* - -

die
the

[80]

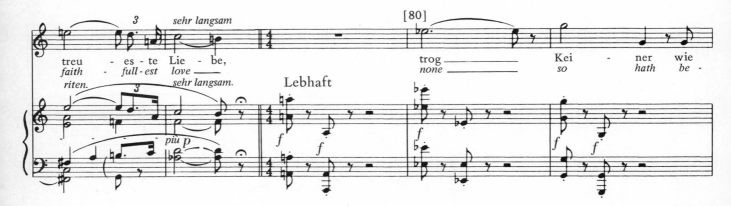

treu - es - te Lie - be,
faith - full - est love
riten. *sehr langsam.*
sehr langsam
più p

Lebhaft

trog
none

Kei - ner wie
so hath be -
f *f*
f *f*
f *f*

198   *Richard Wagner*

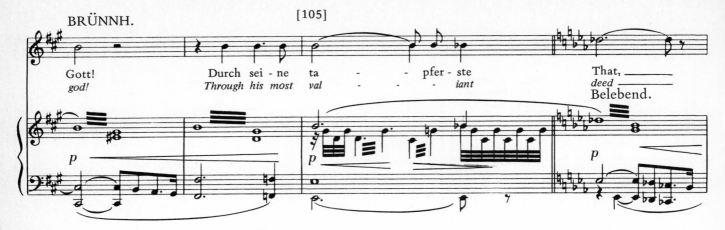

BRÜNNH.

[105]

Gott! Durch sei - ne ta - - pfer - ste That, _____
god! *Through his most val - - iant deed*
Belebend.

[110]

dir _____ so taug - lich er - wünscht, weiht - est du den, ___ der sie ge -
by thee so dear - ly de - sired, didst thou con - demn ___ him to en -

wirkt, dem Flu - che dem du ver - fie - lest,
dure the doom that on thee had fal - len,

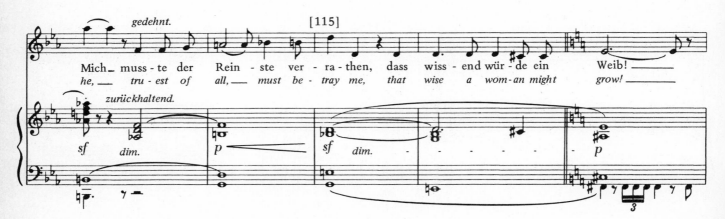

[115]

Mich. ___ muss - te der Rein - ste ver - ra - then, dass wiss - end wür - de ein Weib!
he, ___ tru - est of all, ___ must be - tray me, that wise a wom - an might grow! ___

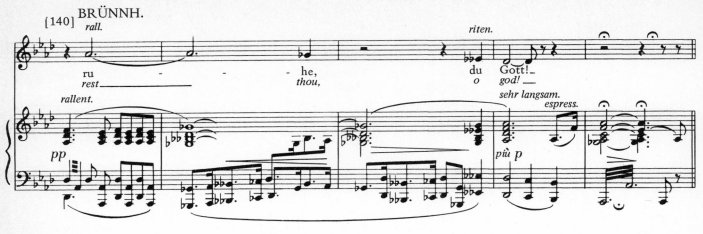

ru — — — he, du Gott!

rest thou, o god!

[145]

(She makes a sign to the Vassals to lift Siegfried's body on to the pyre; at the same time she draws the ring from Sieg-

Voriges Zeitmass, feierlich.

fried's finger looks at it meditatively.)

[150]

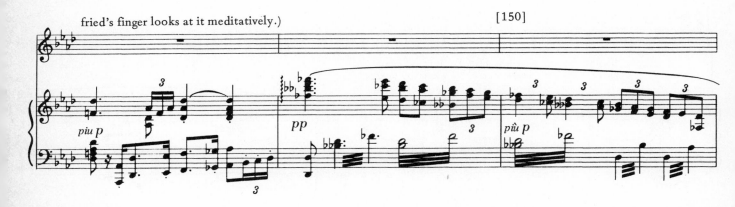

Mein Er-be nun nehm' ich zu ei-gen.   Ver-fluch — ter

My her-i-tage yields now the he-ro.   *Ac-cur — sed*

BRÜNNH.

gehrt ___ ich geb' ___ es euch: aus mei - ner
sire ___ I leave ___ to you: now from my

[175]

As - che nehmt es zu ei - gen! Das Feu - er, das mich ver - brennt, rein' - ge vom
ash - es take ye your treas - ure! Let fire, burn - ing this hand, cleanse, too, the

[180]

Flu - che den Ring! ___ Ihr in der Fluth lö - set ihn
ring from its curse! ___ Ye in the flood, wash it a -

[185]

auf, ___ und lau - ter be - wahrt das lich - te
way, ___ and pur - er pre - serve your shin - ing

204   Richard Wagner

[190]

Gold, das Euch zum Un - - - heil ge - was
gold *that to your sor - - - row was*

[195]

(She has put the ring on her finger and now turns to the pile of logs on which Siegfried's body lies stretched. She takes a great fire-brand from one of the men.)

raubt.
stol'n.

[200]

Lebhaft.

(Waving the fire-brand and pointing to the background.)

Fliegt heim ihr
Fly home ye

BRÜNNH.

Ra - ben!
ra - vens!

Raun't es eu - rem
tell your lord the

f

fp

[205]

Her - ren, was hier am Rhein ihr ge-
ti - dings that here on the Rhine ye have

f

tr

hört! ____
learned! ____

An
To

Noch etwas lebhafter.

f

stacc.

[210]

Brünn - - hil - de's Fel - - sen fahrt vor-
Brünn - - hil - de's rock ____ first wing your

stacc.

fp

cresc.

BRÜNNH.

bei! ____ Der dort noch lo - dert,
flight! ____ *there burn - eth Lo - ge:*

wei - set Lo - ge nach
straight way bid him to

[215]

Wal - hall!
Wal - hall!

Noch etwas gedrängter.

Denn der Göt - ter En - de
For the end of god - hood

[220]

däm - mert nun auf. So ____ werf' ich den
draw - eth now near. *So ____ cast I the*

[225] BRÜNNH.

Brand _____
brand _____

in Wal – hall's
on Wal – hall's

pran – gen – de
glit – ter – ing

(She flings the brand on the wood-pile which quickly breaks out into bright flames.)

[230]

(Two ravens fly up from the rock and disappear in the background.)

Burg.
walls.

stacc.

fp _____ fp _____

stacc.

(Brünnhilde perceives her horse which has just been led in by two men.)

[235]

più f

ff

stacc.

marcato

BRÜNNH.

Gra – ne,
Gra – ne,

mein
my

Ross! _____
steed, _____

fp

p

cresc. - - - - - -

p marcato

[240]

(She has sprung towards him, seizes

and unbridles him: then she bends affectionately towards him.)

Sei mir ge - grüsst!
I greet thee, friend!

[245]

Weisst du auch, mein Freund, wo - hin ich dich
Know'st thou now to whom and whith - er I

füh - re?
lead thee?

Im Feu - er
In fire

BRÜNNH. [250]

leuch-tend,
ra - diant,
liegt
lies
dort dein
there thy
Herr,
lord,

Sieg   -   fried,
Sieg   -   fried,
mein
my
se
he
li - ger
ro ___

[255]

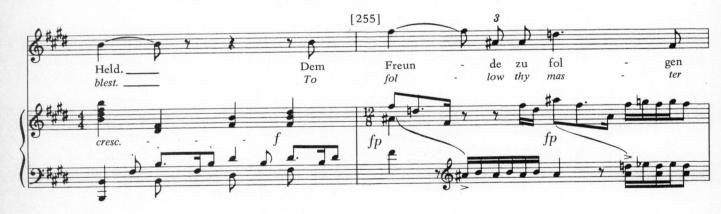

Held. ___
blest. ___
Dem
To
Freun   -   de zu fol   -   gen
fol   -   low thy mas   -   ter

wie   -   herst du freu - dig?
joy   -   ful - ly neigh'st thou?

BRÜNNH.

Lockt____ dich zu ihm____ die la - - chen-de
Lures____ thee to him____ the light____ with its

[260]

Lo - he? Fühl'____ mei - ne
laugh - ter? Feel,____ too, my

Brust auch, wie sie ent - brennt,____ hel - les Feu - er das Herz mir er -
bo - som, how it doth burn;____ glow - ing flames now lay hold on my

[265]

fasst, ihn zu um - schlin - gen, um -
heart: fast to en - fold him, em -

BRÜNNH.

[270]

schlos - sen von ihm, ___ in mäch - tig-ster Min - ne, ver
braced ___ by his arms, ___ in might of our lov - ing with

mählt ___ ihm ___ zu sein! ___ Hei - a - ja-ho! Gra-ne!
him ___ aye ___ made one! ___ Hei - a - ja-ho! Gra-ne!

[275]

(She has swung herself on the horse and urges it to spring

Grüss' ___ dein-en Her - ren! Sieg - fried! Sieg - fried!
Give ___ him thy greet - ing! Sieg - fried! Sieg - fried!

forwards.)

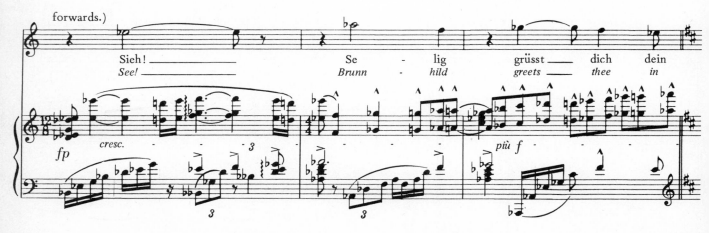

Sieh! ___ Se - lig grüsst ___ dich dein
See! ___ Brünn - hild greets ___ thee in

212   *Richard Wagner*

[280]

BRUNNH. (She makes her horse leap into the burning pile of logs.)

Weib.
bliss.
Die Viertel bedeutend schneller wie vorher.

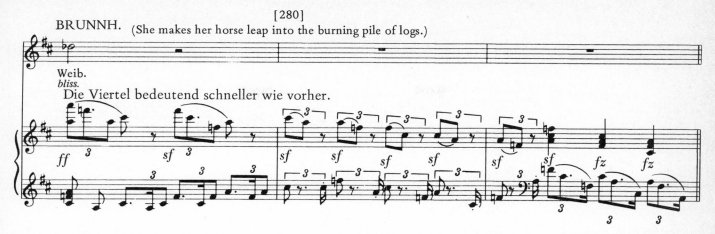

(The flames immediately blaze up so that they fill the whole space in front of the hall, and appear to seize on the build-
Wieder das vorangehende Zeitmass.

ing itself.)

[285]

(The men and women press to the front in terror.)

[290] (As the whole space of the stage seems filled with fire, the glow suddenly subsides, so that only a cloud of smoke re-

mains which is drawn to the background and there lies on the horizon as a dark bank of cloud. At the same time the

[295]

Rhine overflows its banks in a mighty flood which rolls over the fire. On the waves the three Rhine-daughters swim for-

wards and now appear on the place of the fire. Hagen, who since the incident of the ring, has observed Brünnhilde's

behaviour with growing anxiety, is seized with great alarm at the appearance of the Rhine-daughters.)

(He hastily throws spear, shield and helmet from him and rushes, as if mad, into the flood. Woglinde and Wellgunde

HAG.

Zu-rück vom
Give back the

embrace his neck with their arms and draw him with them into the depths as they swim away.)

Ring!
ring!

marcatissimo

ff

sempre ff

poco dim.

[305]

(Flosshilde, swimming in front of the

dim.

p

cresc.

Ped.

others towards the back, holds up the regained ring joyously.)

[310]

(Through the bank of clouds which lie on the horizon a red glow breaks forth with increasing brightness. Illumined

by this light, the three Rhine-daughters are seen, swimming in circles, merrily playing with the ring on the calmer waters

of the Rhine which has gradually returned to its natural bed.)

(From the ruins of the fallen hall, the men and women, in the greatest agitation,

216   *Richard Wagner*

look on the growing fire-light in the heavens. As this at length glows with the greatest brightness, the interior of Wal-

[335]

hall is seen, in which gods and heroes sit assembed, as in Waltraute's description in the first act.—)

[350]

(Bright flames appear to seize on the hall of the gods.)

(As the gods become entirely hidden by the flames, the curtain falls.)
Etwas zurückhaltend.

RIGOLETTO

ACT I, SCENE 1

GIUSEPPE VERDI

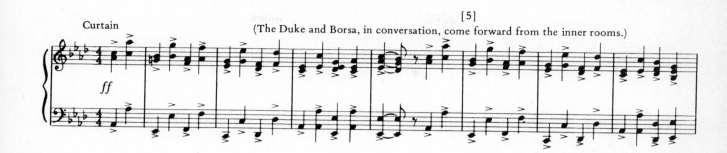

Curtain

[5] (The Duke and Borsa, in conversation, come forward from the inner rooms.)

Duke.

[10]

Del - la mia bel - la in-cog-ni-ta bor - ghe - se toc-ca - re il fin del'av-ven-tu-ra io
This ver - y night I will fin-ish my ad - ven - ture With that young girl I fol-lowed in the

Borsa.

Duke. [15]

vo - glio. Di quel-la gio-vin che ve-de-te al tem - pio? Da tre me - si o - gni
cit - y! Is this the girl you no-ticed Sun-day morn - ing? Ev - 'ry Sun - day for three

Borsa.

Duke. [20]

fe - sta. La sua di - mo - ra? In un re - mo - to cal - le;
months now. Where will you find her? She lives not far from here.

tri - a. Ne sven - tu - ra per me cer - to sa - ri - a.
spite - ful. Then this con - quest would be twice as de - light - ful!

No. 2. "Questa o quella per me pari sono."

Allegretto

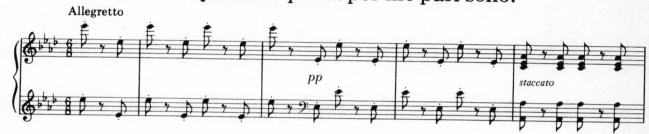

pp
staccato

Duke. *con eleganza*

Que - sta o quel - la_____ per me pa - ri so - no a quan - t'al - tre d'in -
Charm - ing wom - en,_____ What - ev - er their name and rank, I al - ways pur -

tor - no,_____ d'in - tor - no mi ve - do, del mio co - re_____
sue them_____ with e - qual a - ban - don. At my pleas - ure_____

Recitativo and Aria

l'ul - ti - mo mi o so - spir, ca - ro no - me, tuo sa -
heart be - longs. to you a - lone, All my heart for - ev - er

rà!
more!

Col pen - sier il mio de - sir
All my heart is yours a - lone!

a te sem - pre vo - le - rà,
And my love for - ev - er more!

dolce
a tè
Ah,

vo - le - rà, fin l'ul - ti - mo so - spir,
ev - er - more! the mem - 'ry of his name,

fin l'ul - ti - mo so - spir, ca - ro no - me, tuo sa -
its bright and glow - ing flame may light my

ra, ca - - - - - - - - - ro no - me, tuo sa -
soul, ah, _____ my soul for - ev - er -

rà, il mio de - sir a te o - gno - ra
more! My love for you shall nev - er die, shall

vo - le - rà, fin l'ul - ti - mo so - spi - ro
nev - er die, My love for you shall nev - er

tuo _____ sa - - - - - - - - rà!
die, _____ ah _____ no!

(She enters the house, and reappears on the terrace with a lamp to look after her lover down the street.)

Gual - tier Mal - dè!
Gual - tier Mal - dè!

Recitative and Aria.

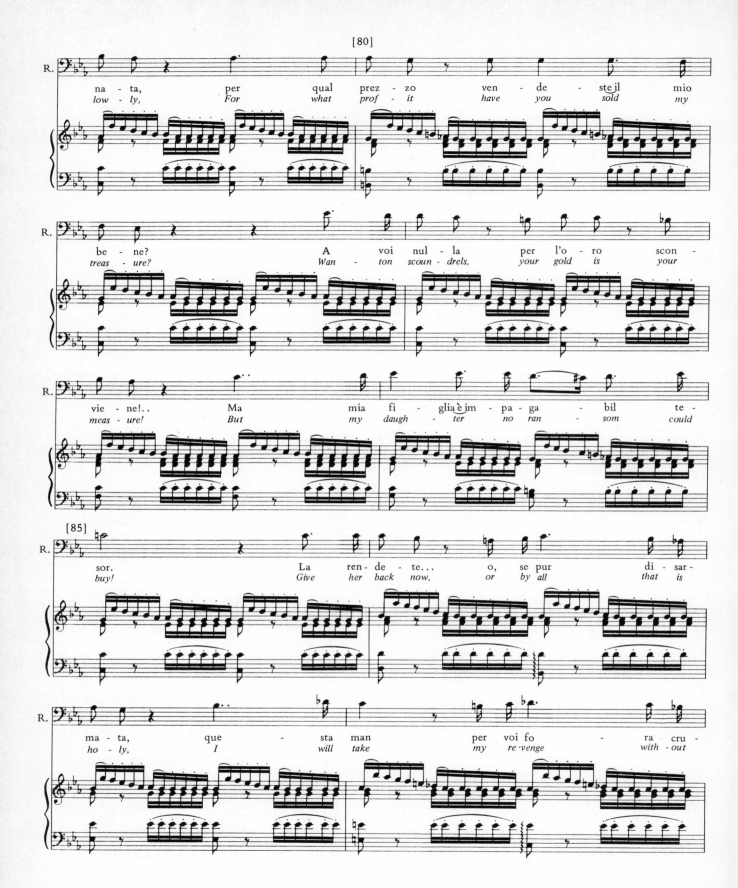

gliar - do la fi - glia ri - da - - te... Ri - do -
treat   you,   have pit - y   on   a   fa - - ther!   Give   her

nar - la a voi nul - la o - ra co - sta,   a voi nul - la o - ra
back,   for   to you   she means noth - ing,   for   to you she means

[120]

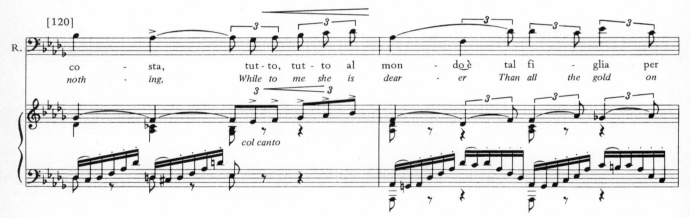

co - sta,   tut - to, tut - to al mon - do è tal fi - glia per
noth - ing,   While to me she is dear - er Than all the gold on

col canto

me.   Si - gno - ri, per - don,   per - do - no, pie -
earth.   Have pit - y,   my lords,   re - store   her to

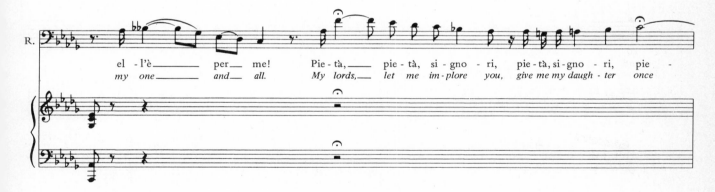

DIE MAINACHT, OP. 43, NO. 2

JOHANNES BRAHMS

wandl' ich trau - rig von Busch zu Busch.
sadly I wander from glade to glade.

[15]

Ü - ber - hül - let vom Laub gir - ret ein Tau - ben-paar sein Ent - zük - ken mir
Hiding deep in the leaves list to the turtle dove softly cooing of

[20]

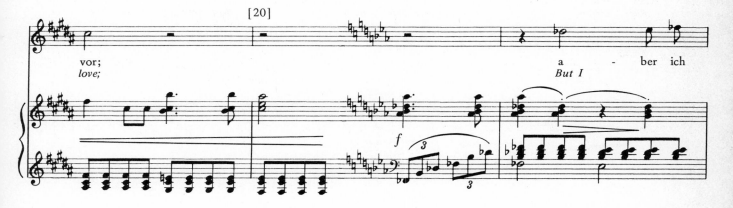

vor; a - ber ich
love; But I

[25]

wen - de mich, su - che dunk - le - re Schat - ten,
turn àway, seek deeper shadows,

Und ... die ein - sa - me Trä - - - - - -
And ... the lonely tear

- - - ne bebt mir hei - sser,
burns

hei - - sser die Wang _____ her -
hotter down _____ my

ab.
cheek.

INTERMEZZO, OP. 116, NO. 5

JOHANNES BRAHMS

Andante con grazia ed intimission sentimento

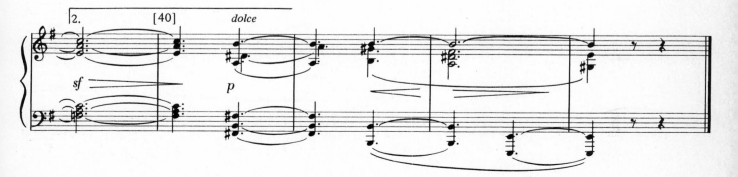

INTERMEZZO, OP. 116, NO. 6

JOHANNES BRAHMS

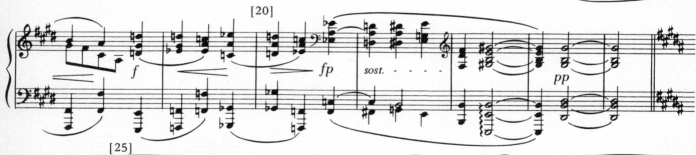

QUINTET, OP. 111

FIRST MOVEMENT

JOHANNES BRAHMS

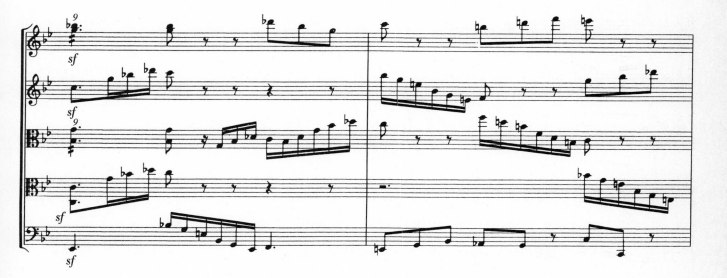

[80]

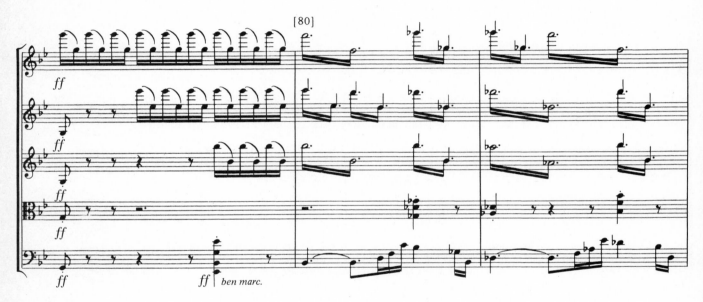

[95]

[100]

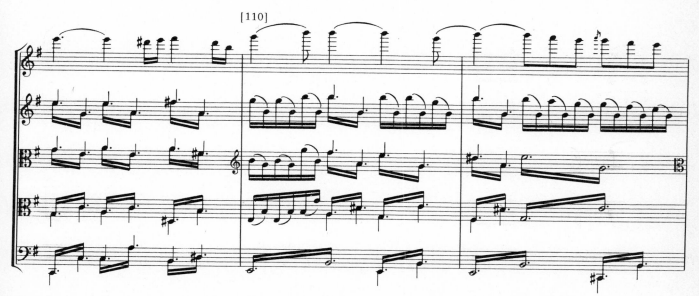

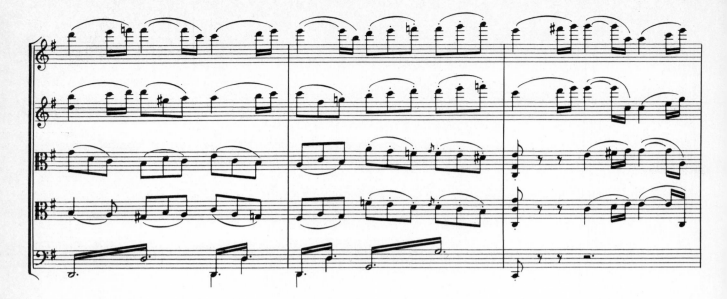

[125]

[130]

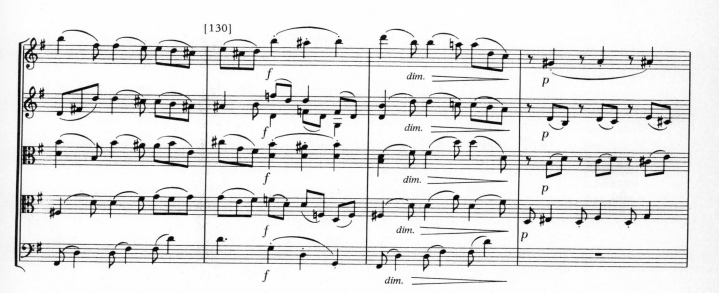

[135]

[140]

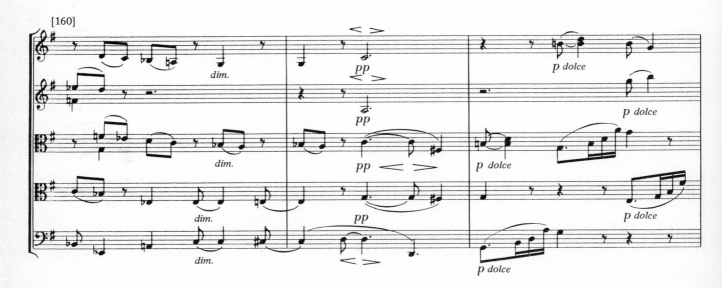

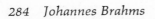

[170]

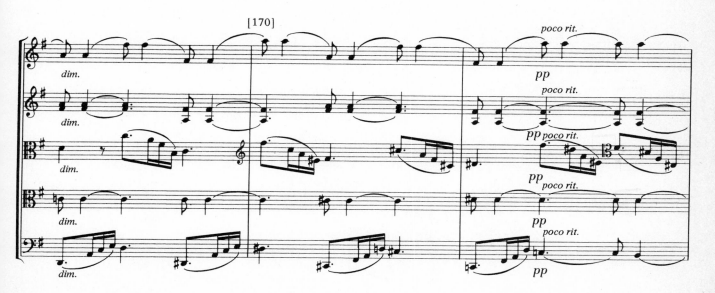

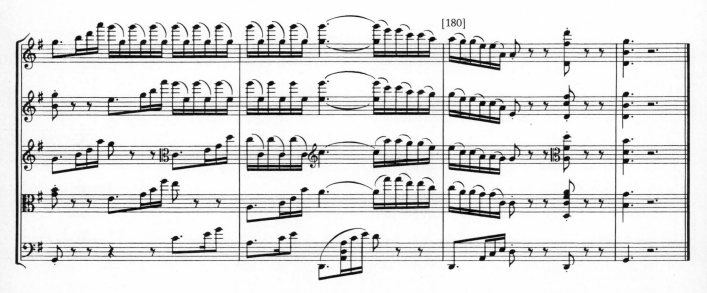

VARIATIONS ON A THEME BY HAYDN

OP. 56b, FOR TWO PIANOS

JOHANNES BRAHMS

Chorale: St. Anthony

Var. 1

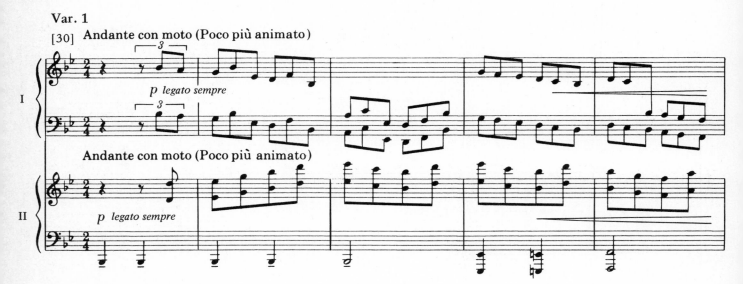

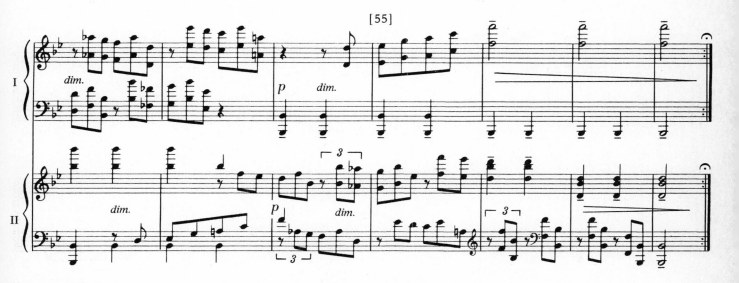

Var. 2 Più vivace

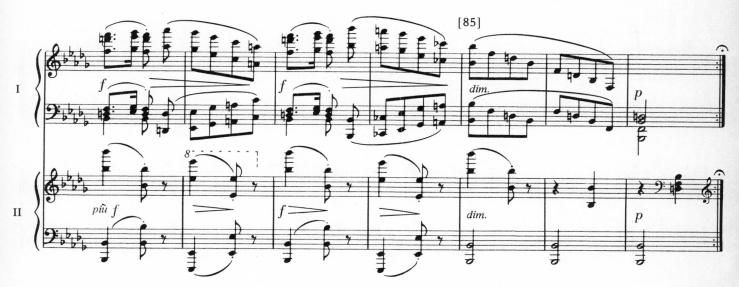

Var. 3

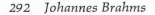

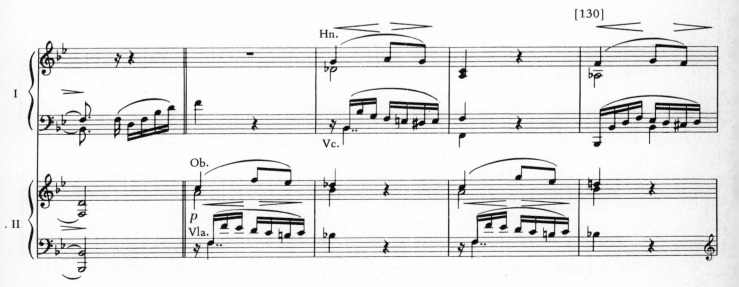

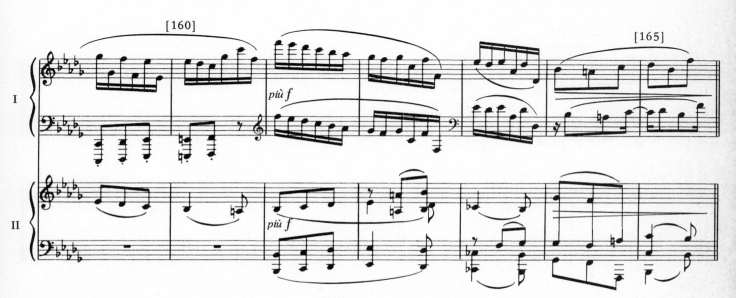

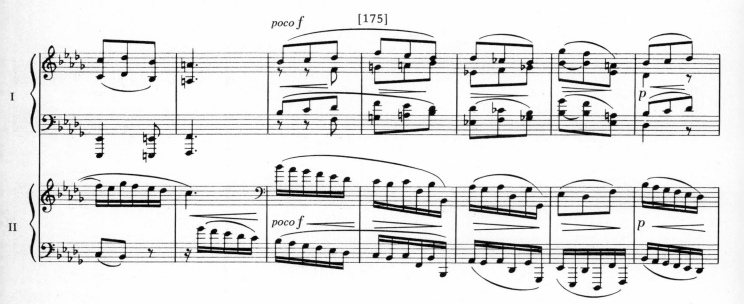

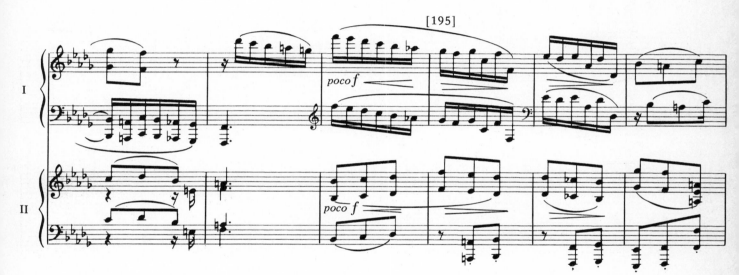

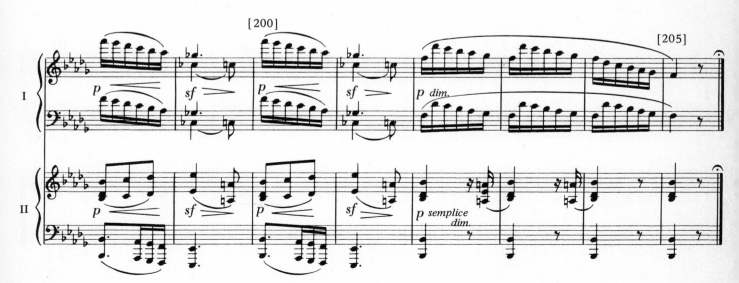

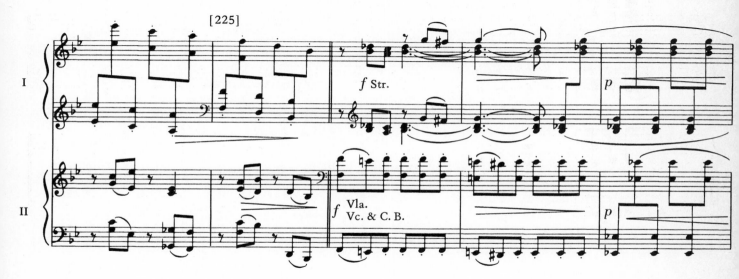

Finale

rit.

EIN DEUTSCHES REQUIEM

IV. HOW LOVELY ARE THY DWELLING PLACES

JOHANNES BRAHMS

* My soul longeth and fainteth . . .

..... for the

Thee everlastingly

CARMEN

DUET AND FINAL CHORUS

GEORGES BIZET

pas ___ j'im - plo - re, je sup - pli - e! No - tre pas - se, ___ Car -
you, ___ I beg you, I en - treat you! I will for - get, ___ Car -

[15]

men, ___ no - tre pas - sé, ___ je l'ou - bli - e! Oui, ___ nous al - lons tous
men, all that has pass'd I will forget it! Yes, ___ let us go to -

[20]

deux ___ Com - men - cer ___ une au - tre vi - e, Loin d'i -
geth er, To begin another life, far from

Carmen.   *mf*

Tu de - man - des l'im - pos - si - ble! Car - men ja - mais n'a men -
What you ask is im - pos - si - ble! Car - men nev - er tells a

ci ___ sous d'au - tres cieux!
here under other skies!

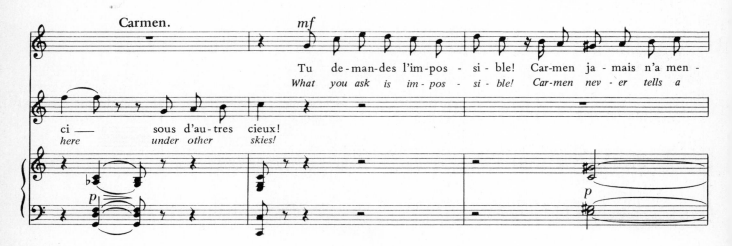

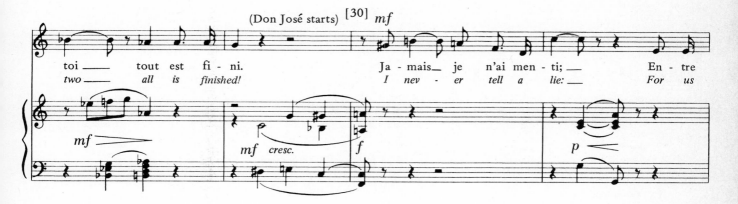

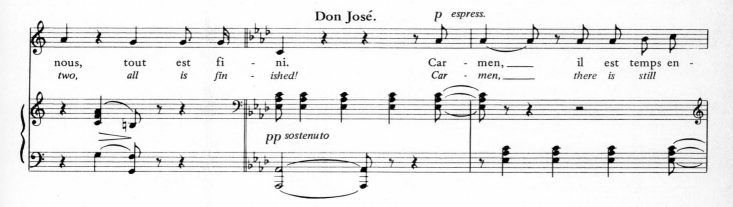

ma Car - men, lais - se - moi te sau - ver, toi que j'a - do - re. Ah!
my Car - men, let me save you, for still I love you. Ah!

lais - se - moi te sau - ver Et me sau - ver a - vec
Let me save you, Save you, and my - self as

Un poco animato
Carmen. *f*

Non! je sais bien que c'est l'heu - re, Je sais
No! well I know that this is the hour, Well I

toi!
well!
Un poco animato

bien que tu me tue - ras;
know that you will kill me;

Mais que je vive ou que je meu - re, Non,_____ non!_____
But if I live, or if I die,_____ No!_____ no!_____

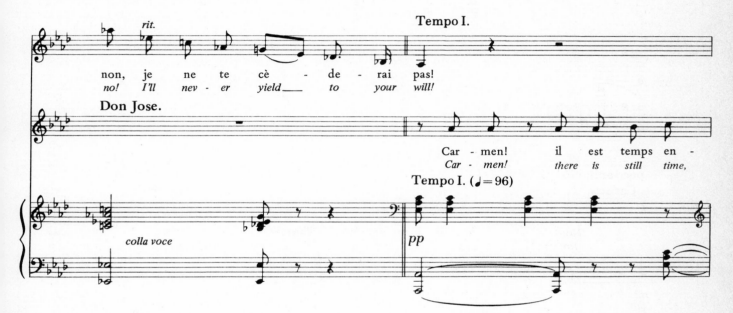

Tempo I.

non, je ne te cè - de - rai pas!
no! I'll nev - er yield_____ to your will!

Don Jose.

Car - men! il est temps en -
Car - men! there is still time,

Tempo I. ($\mathbf{\downarrow}$ = 96)

colla voce   *pp*

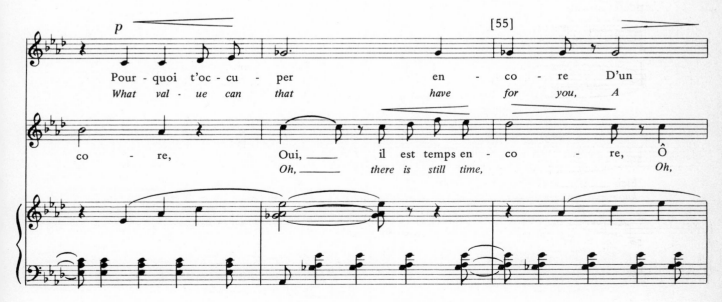

p   [55]

Pour - quoi t'oc - cu - per en - co - re D'un
What val - ue can that have for you, A

co - re, Oui,_____ il est temps en - co - re, Ô
Oh,_____ there is still time, Oh,

coeur qui n'est plus à toi!
heart that is yours no more?

ma Car - men, lais - se - moi Te sau - ver, toi que j'a - do - re! Ah!
my Car - men, let me save you for still I love you! Ah!

[60]

Non, ce coeur n'est plus à toi.
No, this heart is yours no more!

lais - se - moi te sau - ver Et me sau - ver a - vec
let me save you, Save you, and my - self as

En vain tu dis: "Je t'a - dore!" Tu n'ob - tien - dras
In vain you say: "I a - dore you!" I am deaf, how -

toi, Ô ma Car - men, il est temps en - co - re, Ah! lais - se
well, Oh, my Car - men, there is still time, Ah! let me

348   Georges Bizet

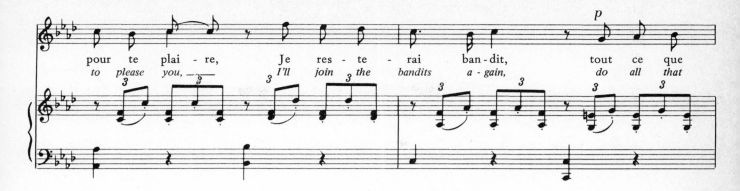

pour te plai - re, Je res - te - rai ban - dit, tout ce que
to please you, I'll join the bandits a - gain, do all that

tu vou - dras Tout! tu m'en - tends, tout, tu m'en -
you de - sire: All! do you hear? all! do you

[95]

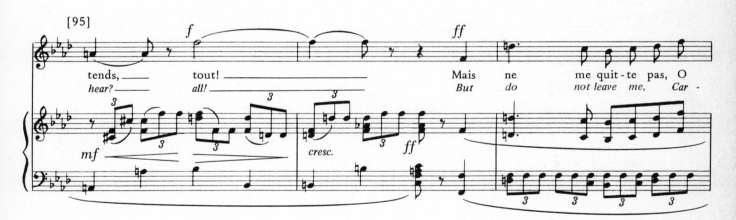

tends, tout! Mais ne me quit - te pas, O
hear? all! But do not leave me, Car -

ma Car - men, Ah! sou - viens - toi, sou - viens - toi
men, Car - men, Ah! but re - call, re - call that

du pas - sé! ____ Nous nous aim - ions, na - guè - re!
time *a - gain!* ____ *We lov'd each other not so long ago!*

Ah! ne me quit - te pas, Car - men, ah! ne me quit - te
Do not for - sake me now, Car - men, do not for - sake me

[105] **Carmen.**

pas! Ja - mais Car - men ____ ne cè - de - ra! ____
now! *Never will Car - men ____ surrender!*

Li - bre elle est née et li - bre el - le mour -
Free she was born, and free will ___ she

(Hearing the cries of the crowd in the amphitheatre, applauding Escamillo, Carmen makes a gesture of delight. — Don José keeps his eyes fixed on her. — At the end of the chorus, Carmen attempts to enter the amphitheatre; but Don José steps in front of her.)

Allegro giocoso.

Chorus.

ra!
die!

Vi - va! vi - va! la course est bel - le! Vi - va! sur le sa - ble san - glant,
Vi - va! vi - va! Glo - ri - ous scene! Ah! Vi - va! On the bloody sand,

Allegro giocoso.

(Fanfare behind the scenes.)

[115]

Le tau - reau, le tau - reau s'é - lan - ce! Voy - ez, voy - ez, voy - ez, voy -
How the bull, the bull mad - ly rush - es! See there! see there! see there! see

[120]

ez! ___ Le tau - reàu qu'on har - cèle En bon - dis - sant s'é - lan - ce, Voy - ez!
there! ___ The bull, tormented In great leaps he rush - es! See there!

Molto moderato. (♩ = 84)

Je l'aime et de-vant la mort mê-me Je ré-pè-te-rai que je l'ai -
I love him and before death itself, I'd say again that I love

[150] Allegro giocoso. (Carmen again tries to enter the amphitheatre, Don José stops her again.)

me!
him!

Chorus.

Vi - va! vi - va! la course est bel - le! Vi - va! sur le sa - ble san-glant,
Vi - va! vi - va! glo - ri - ous scene! ah! Vi - va! on the bloody sand,

Allegro giocoso.

(Fanfare behind the scenes.)

[155]

I.

Le tau-reau, le tau-reau s'é-lan - ce! Voy-ez, voy - ez, voy-ez, voy -
How the bull, the bull mad-ly rush-es! See there! see there! see there! see

ALL

Voy - ez, voy - ez, voy -
See there! see there! see

ez! — Le tau - reau qu'on harcèle En bon - dis - sant s'é - lan - ce, voy - ez!
there! The bull, tormented, A - cross the ring he rush - es, see there!

Moderato.   Don Jose.

Ain - si,   le sa - lut de mon â - me   Je l'au rai per-du   pour que
so,   the hope of my life   I   will lose   because

(Orchestra) *ff*   *colla voce*

fp

a tempo   Recit.

toi, ___   Pour que tu t'en ail - les, in - fâ - me, En - tre ses
you ___   because you love him,   you   wretch,   In   his

ff a tempo   *colla voce*

fp

a tempo.

[170]   *ff un poco animato.*

bras ri - re de moi!   Non, par le sang, tu n'i - ras   pas!   Car-men,
arms to laugh at me!   No, by my life,   It shall not   be!   Car-men,

ff a tempo

fp   *ff*

Don José.

(rushing towards Carmen.)

fois, tu me l'a-vais don-né-e, Tiens! Eh bien! dam-né-e!

bought, the one that you gave me, So! You will! be damned!

ff a tempo *colla voce* *ff (Fanfare behind the scenes.)*

(Carmen attempts to escape, but Don José catches up with her at the entrance of the amphitheatre; he stabs her; she falls, and dies.)

[190] **Chorus in unison and octaves.**

To - re - a - dor, en gar - de! ___ To - re - a - dor! ___

To - re - a - dor, make read - y, ___ To - re - a - dor! ___

(Orchestra) *espress.*

[195]
(Don José, distracted, falls on his knees beside her.)

To - re - a - dor! ___ Et son - ge bien, oui songe en com - bat - tant, ___

To - re - a - dor! ___ And think well, remember in combat, ___

Qu'un oeil noir te re - gar - de, Et que l'a - mour t'at - tend,

that a dark eye watches you, And that love a - waits you,

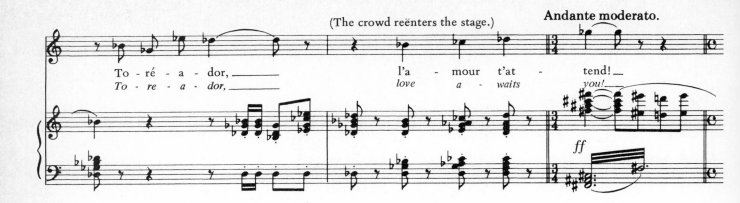

(The crowd reënters the stage.)

Andante moderato.

To - ré - a - dor, _____ l'a - mour t'at - tend! _____

To - re - a - dor, _____ love a - waits you! _____

ff

Don José. *f*

Vous pou - vez m'ar - rê - ter. _____ C'est moi _____ qui l'ai tu -

Do with me what you will, _____ I'm the one who killed her!

fp *ff* *fp*

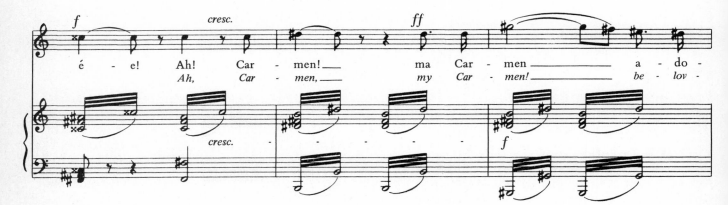

f *cresc.* *ff*

é - e! Ah! Car - men! _____ ma Car - men _____ a - do -

Ah, Car - men, _____ my Car - men! _____ be - lov -

cresc. *f*

(Curtain.)

ré - e!

ed! _____

f *p* *f* *p* *ff*

BORIS GODUNOV

CORONATION SCENE

MODESTE MUSSORGSKY

A square in the Moscow Kremlin. Facing the audience, up-stage, the Great Staircase
of the Imperial Palace. Right, down-stage, the crowd is kneeling in the space between
the Cathedral of the Assumption, (right) and the Cathedral of the Archangels (left, dis-
tant). The porches of both Cathedrals are visible. Solemn peals of bells.

Mussorgsky's original version, not revision and recomposition by Rimsky-Korsakov

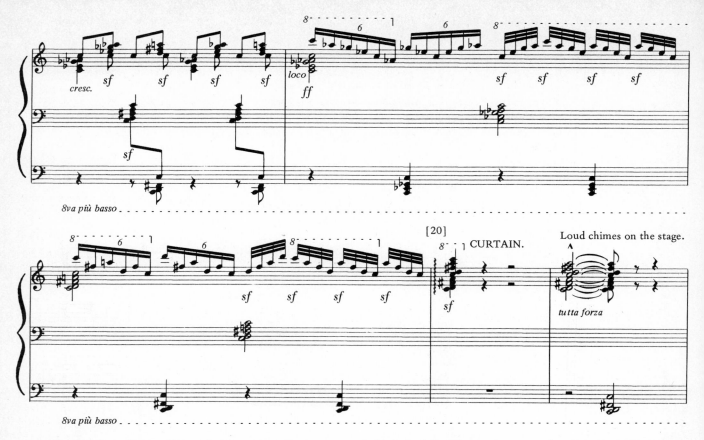

[20] CURTAIN.

Loud chimes on the stage.

From the Great Staircase boyars in solemn procession start towards the Cathedral of the Assumption; in front are guards, Strelstsy,

and boyar children; then comes Shuisky, carrying the crown of Monomach on a cushion. Behind him boyars, Shchelkalov carrying

the Imperial sceptre; then more Strelstsy, the chief boyars, the secretaries, etc. The procession passes among the crowd and enters the

Cathedral of the Assumption. The Strelstsy stand in files on both sides of the steps.

[35]

8va più basso

SHUISKY, appearing in the porch
[40]
ff
Long

The chimes on the stage continue.

Tpts. ff

of the Cathedral of the Assumption; to the crowd.

life to our Tsar Bo-ris Fe - o-do-ro-vich!

The crowd stands up.

f cresc.

[60]

glo - ry, glo - ry, O - ver Rus - sia our Tsar Bo - ris now

glo - ry, glo - ry, O - ver Rus - sia our Tsar Bo - ris now

[65] The Tsar's procession comes out of the

reigns _ in glo - ry, glo - ry!

reigns _ in glo - ry, glo - ry!

Basses *pp*

Long

Cathedral of the Assumption. The police officers marshal the people into rows.

Trumpeters take place facing the audience, in front of the crowd.

Shchelkalov and the boyars follow the procession, and form a semi-circle line extending from the Cathedral of the Archangels to the

O - ver Rus - sia Bo - ris ___ now reigns ___ in

etc.

[105] Cathedral of the Assumption.

glo - ry, ___ glo - ry, ___ reigns in ___ glo - ry!

Boris appears in the Cathedral porch. Shuisky, behind the Tsar's back, signals to the people to keep silence, and with Vorotynsky

[110]

Glo - ry! glo - ry! glo - ry! glo - ry!

T. B.

Glo - ry! glo - ry! glo - ry!

takes his place behind Boris. The chimes cease.

Glo - ry! glo - ry! glo - ry! glo - ry!

BORIS. From the porch; his children, Feodor and Xenia, are behind him.

Meno mosso
[115]

My soul is sad! A se-cret ter - ror

[120]

haunts me; with e - vil pre-sen - ti-ments my heart is stif - led. O Lord a-bove,

In mood of exaltation.

[125]

O Thou Al-might - y Fa - ther! From Heav - en's throne be-hold our con - trite

tears, and with your bless - ing grant me ho - li - ness and strength, that they may guide me.

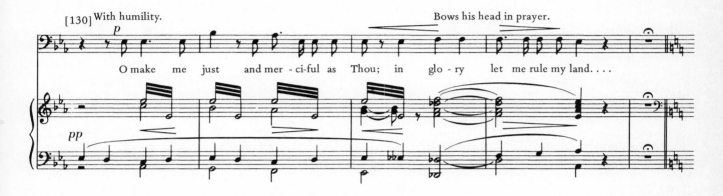

[130] With humility.   Bows his head in prayer.

O make me just and mer - ci - ful as Thou; in glo - ry let me rule my land. . . .

[135] Raising his head, sternly.

Now let us kneel and pay our hom - age at the tombs of Rus-sia's mon-archs.

Majestically.   [140]

And then our peo - ple all shall feast,   yea, ev - 'ry

man,   from boy-ar down to   serf;   all   shall we greet,   all ____ glad-ly shall we wel-come!

Boris, accompanied by Shuisky and Vorotinsky, comes down the steps. The boyars and Streltsy follow. The procession proceeds

Glo-ry,   glo-ry, glo - ry!   Long live our sovereign,

towards the Cathedral of the Archangels.

The people rush towards the Cathedral.

The police maintain order.

Tsar of Rus - sia!   Hon - our and   glo - ry   to you our fa - ther!

Chimes only

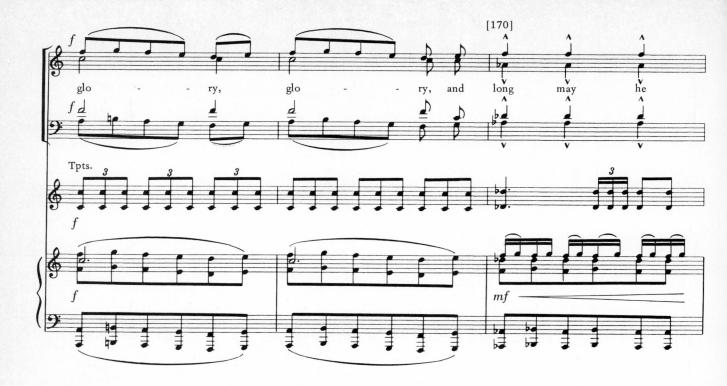

glo — ry, glo — ry, and long may he

pros — per!   Tumult. The police struggle with the crowd.

Boris comes out of the Cathedral of the Archangels and proceeds towards the palace.

Glo - ry! Glo - ry, glo - ry, glo - ry!

Glo - ry, glo - ry!

CURTAIN.

EXTASE

HENRI DUPARC

Lento e tranquillo *(Lent et calme)*

On   a   pale   lil   -   y
Sur   un lys   pâ   -   le

is   my   rest,   and my slum   -   ber   like death is
mon   coeur dort   D'un som-meil   doux   com - me la

IN DEM SCHATTEN MEINER LOCKEN

HUGO WOLF

Leicht, zart, nicht schnell
(In a light, delicate style and not too fast)

In dem Schat - ten mei - ner Lo - cken schlief mir mein Ge - lieb - ter
In the shad - ow of my tress - es, my be - loved to sleep has

ein.   Weck ich ihn nun auf? _____
gone.   *Shall I wake him now?* _____

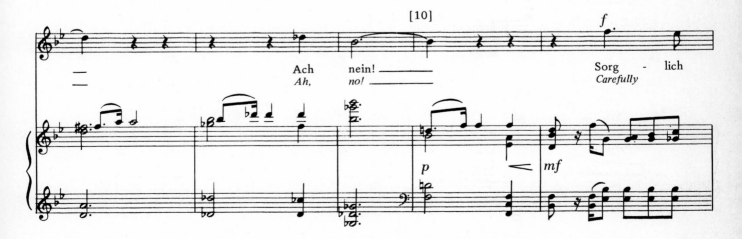

Ach nein! _____ Sorg - lich
Ah, no! _____ *Carefully*

strählt ich mei - ne krau - sen Lo - cken täg - lich in der Frü - he,
I combed my curly tresses daily in the morning.

[15]

doch um - sonst ist mei - ne Mü - he, weil die Win - de sie zer -
all in vain, is my effort, for the winds my locks dis-

[20]

sau - sen.
hev - elled.

poco rit. 3 [25]

Lo - cken - schat - ten, Win - des - sau - sen schlä - fer - ten den Lieb - sten ein.
The shadow of my tresses, the wind's sighing lulled my love to sleep.

Weck ich ihn nun auf? —
Shall I waken him? —

Ach
Ah,

nein! —
no! —

Hö - ren muss ich, wie ihn grä - me, dass er
I'm obliged to listen, how worried he is, that he

schmach - tet schon so lan - ge, dass ihm Le - ben geb und
yearned for me so long, that life is given to him and

neh - me die - se mei - ne brau - ne Wan - ge.
taken away by my brown cheek.

Und er nennt mich sei - ne
And he calls me his

Schlan - ge, und doch schlief er bei mir ein.
ser - pent, and yet he sleeps at my side.

[45] *molto riten.*   3   *a tempo*

Weck ich ihn nun auf? _____ Ach nein! _____
Shall I wake him now? _____ Ah, no! _____

[50]

[55]

ANAKREONS GRAB

HUGO WOLF

Sehr langsam und ruhig
(Very slowly and quietly)

zart (tenderly)

Wo die Ro - se hier blüht, ___ wo
Where the ro - ses still bloom, ___ where

Re - ben und Lor - beer sich schlin - gen, wo das Tur - tel - chen lockt, ___
vines round the lau - rels are twin - ing, where the dove soft - ly woos, ___

wo sich das Grill - chem er - götzt, ___ welch ein Grab ist hier, das al -
and where the cri - cket is glad, ___ o what grave lies here, that ___ all ___

- le Göt - ter mit Le - - - - ben schön be - pflanzt ___ und ge -
the Gods ___ with ev - - - - er - green have planted ___ and a -

WIE LANGE SCHON

HUGO WOLF

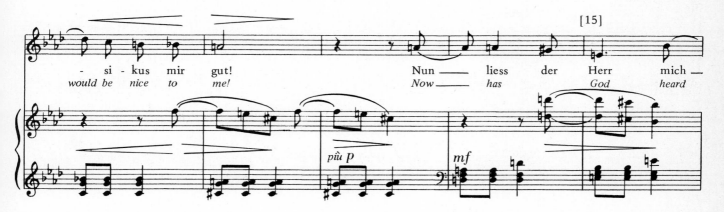

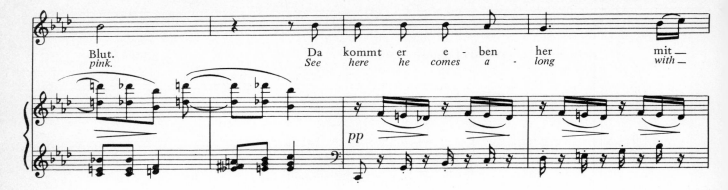

Blut.
pink.
Da kommt er e - ben her mit —
See here he comes a - long with —

[25]

sanf - ter Mie - ne, und senkt den Kopf und
gen - tle mien and bows his head and

[30]
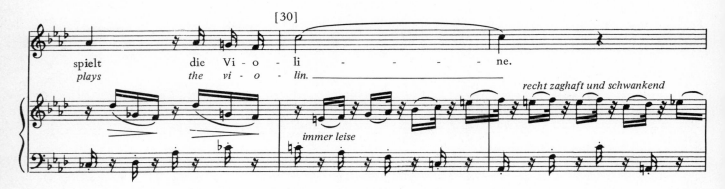

spielt die Vi - o - li - ne.
plays the vi - o - lin.

recht zaghaft und schwankend
immer leise

[35]

zögernd
(langsamer Triller)
tr